BORING

MICHAEL KELLEY

BORING

FINDING AN EXTRAORDINARY GOD
IN AN ORDINARY LIFE

B&H
PUBLISHING GROUP
NASHVILLE, TENNESSEE

Published by B&H Publishing Group
Nashville, Tennessee

Dewey Decimal Classification: 248.84
Subject Heading: CHRISTIAN LIFE \ GOD \ SAUL,
KING OF ISRAEL

1 2 3 4 5 6 7 8 • 17 16 15 14 13

DEDICATION

To Gary, Eric, and Jeffrey Kelley—Three men who show daily that there is no such thing as an ordinary life when you follow an extraordinary God.

CONTENTS

ACKNOWLEDGMENTS

When you come to a publisher with a book that you want to call *Boring*, it makes you very thankful for a partner in ministry that believes in you. I continue to remain grateful and indebted to the good and hard-working people at B&H Publishing. Selma, thank you for believing in me, and for continuing to give me opportunities to flesh out my heart on paper. Jed and Devin, thank you both for the constant encouragement and for helping me to be a better writer.

So many of the ideas expressed in this book are the result of conversations, sermons, and Sunday school classes I've been a part of at Grace Community Church. It would be difficult for me to express how formative living in the midst of this community of faith has been.

I'm particularly grateful to Scott Patty and the team of elders who have shown me, through word and deed, how to find the great beauty, wonder, and significance right square in the middle of everyday life. It is my hope and prayer that we would continue together to do the next right thing.

And Jana—my great love. My bride. The one who has constantly been my biggest cheerleader. There's no one in the world with whom I'd rather find the joy, excitement, and satisfaction of life in Jesus Christ.

AN ORDINARY STORY

Once upon a time, there was an ordinary man. Every day, his alarm clock went off. On good days, he would reach over, turn off the alarm, get up, and go to the gym. On the other days, he would hit the snooze button. Upon returning from the YMCA (or waking up after another hour), this man would take a shower and put on a collared shirt and khaki pants.

He would then hear the scurrying of little feet upstairs, and would trace the sound until it eventually made its way down the stairs revealing three young children hungry for breakfast. The man and his wife would go upstairs and get out bowls, milk, and cereal.

The family would eat and then clean up the dishes. Then he would get in his car and begin the commute to work. When he got to work, just when he thought this was going to be an ordinary day in his ordinary life . . .

It was. He spent the next eight hours sitting in front of his computer. Answering e-mails. Taking phone calls. Checking a news website occasionally. Then he got in his car and went home. When he pulled in, sure that he knew exactly what was going to happen when he opened the back door . . .

He was right again. He hugged and played with all the kids. He kissed his wife. They had dinner. They watched TV. They went to bed.

Yawn.

What did you expect? International intrigue? A call from the president? A natural disaster, or a chance to be a hero? Not here. Not in that day. Not in my life.

Probably not in yours either.

This is what most of my days look like. Oh sure, there is the occasional interruption in the routine and some vacations peppered in there, but by and large, it's a fairly regular way to live. A fairly regular way to live for a fairly regular guy.

Most of us are just that—regular. Ordinary. *Boring.* Most of our lives are spent doing regular, ordinary, boring kinds of things. Changing diapers. Going to work. Reading books. Playing with kids. Relating to our spouses. Paying bills.

I've never met a president. Or saved a child from a burning building. Or climbed Everest. I don't run in powerful circles or tweet nuggets of wisdom adored by millions. My office walls don't have pictures with me and the Queen of England or medals from my wins at the Olympic Games. Perhaps if I were an international man of mystery, I'd look over and see a picture of me standing next to a world leader at that ceremony when I was awarded some token for my bravery. Then I could turn and see another wall full of mementos and trinkets collected from my adventures. Instead I'm looking at four family pictures, a calendar, and a particularly fierce-looking rendering of a black and yellow fire-breathing dragon laying waste to a castle.

Ah, parenthood.

A regular life isn't bad, necessarily. In fact, a certain kind of bliss accompanies the "normal" life. There aren't a lot of surprises, and for a guy who has a to-do list for every day (with the last item on that list being "Make tomorrow's list"), a lack of surprises can be very comforting. What is more, an ordinary life actually affords an opportunity to love things like pictures from an eight-year-old of dragons and castles. In an ordinary life, your existence becomes papered with moments like these.

And yet . . .

And yet there are those days that just feel boring. The routine becomes monotony, and you find yourself refreshing your e-mail over and over again, waiting for something—anything—to break up the ticking of the clock. You feel something inside of you, something that appreciates the life you have, but at the same time wonders if there's something more. Something that you're missing. I feel that way sometimes.

Searching for Significance

The truth is that we will all spend 90 percent of our time here on earth just doing life. Just being ordinary. If this were a self-help book, I might follow that realistic, slightly de-motivating statement up with something like: "Break out of the ordinary. Pursue your bliss. Go skydiving. Do something important. *Carpe diem*." The same motivation, in Christian terms, might read: "God's will is that you have a life of adventure. Get out there and make an eternal difference. Do something big for God."

All of those statements are true in a sense; all of them can be appropriate. What those statements communicate is that we should be focused on Jesus and expanding His kingdom. That should be our priority. Those statements challenge us to recognize that we only have a limited time here on earth, so we need to make sure we spend our time doing things that matter. However, implicit in an exhortation like "do something big for God" is the notion that we are currently *not* doing stuff that matters, and we have to abandon that insignificant stuff to break out of the rut—chase the dream . . . be the man . . . overcome obscurity . . . all that stuff.

Chasing dreams isn't the problem. Neither is maximizing what you have to make a difference in the world for the sake of Christ. The problem is in our definition of significance.

People tend to believe that the pathway to significance is paved with the big, the showy, and the grand. The people who are most often lauded as influential are the ones doing the big, impressive things with their lives. Consequently, those same people cannot involve themselves in these mundane details of life. Indeed, the mundane details are like anchors that weigh a person down from the bigger and the better. So moving toward a life that matters involves moving past the details that don't.

But what if we're wrong? What if "bigness" is not an accurate measure of significance? What if the whole idea of "ordinary" is a myth? And what if a life of great importance isn't found by escaping the details but embracing them? What if God actually doesn't want you to escape from the ordinary, but to find significance and meaning inside of it?

That's what this book is about. This book is for the stay-at-home mom and the office job dad. It's for the regular church member and the ordinary citizen. It's for the person who has ever looked at the seemingly mundane details of life and wondered if they are really doing anything that's worthwhile. It's for all of us ordinary people who are following an extraordinary God. My hope, as you read the first half of this book, is that you would be awakened to the myth of the ordinary as you see and extraordinary God who is constantly moving and working. Then, as you move into the second half of this book, I pray that you might see the greater purposes in a few specific, but often ordinary, areas of life that we tend to push to the margin. And maybe, when we get to the end, we will have begun to see God, and life, in a whole new way. Perhaps we will have begun to see that there really is no such thing as ordinary when you are following an extraordinary God.

CHAPTER 1

CHASING DONKEYS

The Fear of the Ordinary

I am afraid.

There, I said it, and now it's out there. But I need to clarify the statement. My biggest fear in life is not of sickness, financial hardship, public speaking, heights, or even spiders. My biggest fear is being ordinary. I am deathly afraid of being just another guy who blended into the crowd—someone who never did anything important or significant with his life. I am terrified of "eking" my way through life, so caught up in the rut of the mundane that I pass from this Earth as just another inconsequential guy who had a job, raised some kids, and tried to get enough fiber in his diet.

Oh, I don't always feel this way. Every once in a while something exciting rolls into the schedule. But most days are pretty much the same. It's on those days, as I stare at the computer screen or pay the bills, as I have the same wrestling match with my kids or eat the same dinner with my wife—those are the days when I find myself wondering if I'm really doing anything that matters. If I'm really doing anything important at all.

And where does God fit into this equation? During those days, the days of the rut and the treadmill, I find myself wondering if He does at all. Surely this couldn't be what God wants for me, this God who says that He put on flesh to come and give regular folks like me not only life, but life in abundance (John 10:10). So where is it? In my Google Calendar? In my morning commute? In the pancakes I flip every Saturday morning?

I want to propose an idea to you. It's one that's so very simple that we can often miss it. It's an idea that can, I believe, dramatically change the way we view life as a whole:

What if there is no such thing as ordinary?

What if we are looking so hard for these grandiose experiences of significance that we are missing the opportunities for significance right in front of us? What if there is no such thing as ordinary when you follow an extraordinary God?

But don't just take my word for it. Let me tell you a story—a story that actually involves political intrigue, espionage, and matters of national importance. Be warned though—it's a story that also involves donkeys.

The Curious Case of the Missing Donkeys

"Give us a king like the other nations have!" That was the demand of the elders of Israel in 1 Samuel 8, a demand that had been a long time in the making.

Israel had never had a king. They had leaders, for sure. Moses guided them out of Egypt and through the desert wanderings. Joshua led them into the promised land and through the years of conquest. The judges were empowered by God to deliver the Israelites from the hands of their oppressors. Read through the book of Judges, and you can see why the elders would make their request for a king. This is how that period of time is described: "In those days there was no king in Israel; everyone did whatever he wanted" (Judg. 21:25).

These were days of spiritual anarchy with each one determining what was right and wrong for themselves. Perhaps it was a situation not that far from the culture in which we find ourselves today, when truth is relative to a given situation and there is no accepted universal standard of right and wrong.

But the Lord had a plan.

That plan came to fruition in the life of a young boy named Samuel. Samuel was a true prophet; as it says in 1 Samuel, he heard the voice of the Lord and none of His words fell to the ground. Under the leadership of Samuel, Israel enjoyed a period of relative peace and prosperity.

But when we join Samuel's story in 1 Samuel 8, a problem was brewing. Samuel was getting old. What is more, his sons were wicked and not worthy of national leadership (1 Sam. 8:3). That sets up the crisis of leadership that we find in 1 Samuel 8. And that's the backdrop of the demand of the elders of the land brought before Samuel.

"We're tired of this. Give us a king like the other nations have."

Their request may not seem like a big deal, but at its core it was a wicked demand. By demanding a king, the nation was rejecting God. One of the ways God set the nation of Israel—His chosen people—apart from the other nations was that they were to have no earthly king. They would have leaders, but God was their king. This was one of their marks of distinction. But now they were discontent with their lot. They were tired of other nations having a visible, national ruler. They were jealous of them. They wanted what they were never supposed to have.

We can sympathize with the elders, can't we? We long for good leadership in the workplace, in the family, or in the nation. We want to know we can trust those in leadership, trust that they're working for the good of the people or the family. Israel's elders were trying to make a plan for the future. They wanted to make sure the nation was strong for the future, but they knew that if the nation followed its current path, dangers were looming. They also wanted to provide for future generations. Understandable, yes; but just because we understand something doesn't mean it's right.

There was no doubt these were extraordinary times. They were times of national crisis. They were days of cultural definition. They were moments that charted the course of history. But flip the page to 1 Samuel 9, and you don't find the extraordinary. You don't find the political maneuvering or the Oval Office conversations. You know what you do find? A farm-raised country bumpkin, barely five miles away from where Israel's destiny-altering conversation was taking place, whose biggest concern at the moment was some missing donkeys:

> There was a Benjamite, a man of standing, whose name was Kish son of Abiel, the son of Zeror, the son of Bekorath, the son of Aphiah of Benjamin. Kish had a son named Saul, as handsome a young man as could be found anywhere in Israel, and he was a head taller than anyone else.

Now the donkeys belonging to Saul's father
Kish were lost, and Kish said to his son Saul,
"Take one of the servants with you and go and
look for the donkeys." So he passed through the
hill country of Ephraim and through the area
around Shalisha, but they did not find them.
They went on into the district of Shaalim, but
the donkeys were not there. Then he passed
through the territory of Benjamin, but they did
not find them.

When they reached the district of Zuph,
Saul said to the servant who was with them,
"Come, let's go back, or my father will stop
thinking about the donkeys and start worrying
about us." (1 Sam. 9:1–5 NIV)

Talk about boring. It's hard to think of a more dramatic difference between the two chapters. We go from the heights of political intrigue and national crisis to a search for some lost livestock. While Saul was looking high and low for his animals, we start to get some clues from the text that something extraordinary is going on behind the scenes.

This young man was handsome. As handsome as any other man in the land. And he was tall. Interestingly, this is the only time that the adjective tall is applied to an Israelite. He had a commanding stature fit for a king. Heck, his name *Saul* actually means "asked for"!

So you've got a tall, good-looking corn-fed stud named "asked for." Sounds a lot like a king to me.

And yet he's not the sharpest knife in the drawer. He, at this point, has no idea that anything beyond his own scope of vision was happening. He was, in his own mind, doing something completely ordinary. Something radically mundane. Something excruciatingly boring. He was chasing donkeys around the countryside. But his chase led him to an area of the land called Zuph, the domain of Samuel. Thus the stage is set for the collision of the ordinary with the extraordinary.

An Extraordinary Series of Coincidences

What follows is a crazy series of events. Saul wanted to go home, but his servant happened to know about a man of God who lived around there and knew about stuff like lost donkeys. The servant also happened to have a quarter of a shekel to pay the man of God for information.

Now this man of God traveled a lot, but he happened to be in residence as Saul and the servant went walking up the road. And some women happened to be walking out of the town at the same time Saul and his servant were walking up. They happened to know that this man of God was not only in town, but was only a little ways ahead of them on that very road.

Keep in mind, though, that Saul had no idea who Samuel was—or perhaps who the Lord was, for that matter. But the work of God is not dependent on the knowledge or awareness of man. Just the day before, God had whispered to His servant Samuel that the man He would appoint as the leader over Israel was going to show up at just the right time:

> Now the day before Saul's arrival, the LORD had informed Samuel, "At this time tomorrow I will send you a man from the land of Benjamin. Anoint him ruler over My people Israel. He will save them from the hand of the Philistines because I have seen the affliction of My people, for their cry has come to Me." When Samuel saw Saul, the LORD told him, "Here is the man I told you about; he will rule over My people." (1 Sam. 9:15–17)

Pretty amazing series of coincidences, isn't it? It's a lot of things happening in just the right order at just the right time. It almost makes you believe that there actually is no such thing as coincidence at all. If that was true in Saul's life, then maybe it's true in your and mine too. Can you entertain the notion that right now, the same God who whispered in the ear of Samuel is still working in ways you aren't aware of? Maybe even right in the middle of something that seems extremely ordinary? If you can accept that as a possibility, then it can change your perspective on virtually any circumstance in your life.

If we stop to think about it, we can trace most anything in our lives back to seemingly coincidental circumstances. I met my wonderful wife, Jana, in 1997, when we were entering college. Up until a month earlier, I had planned to go to Texas Tech, but then I decided at the last minute to go to a different school. Some years before that, I had met Jana's sisters and brothers-in-law through our church. They, some years before that, decided to go to the same school where they had both met their spouses. Then they all got jobs and decided to stay in the town where they went to school instead of moving away.

You can do the same thing with something as simple as this book you're holding. Did you happen to just be reading this book right now? You might say yes. But if you believe in the sovereignty of God, you can start to trace a line of decisions and circumstances back and back and back and begin to see the remarkable events that came together for this very moment. Right now. Think about it. It will make your head spin.

Did you order the book online? If so, did someone tell you the title? Who was that person? How did you know them? What's your history with them? Did you walk into a bookstore? What was it about this book that caught your eye? Did the cover intrigue you? Perhaps because it struck a chord with something in your past? See how it works?

The work of God wasn't dependent on Saul's awareness of that work. Neither is God's work dependent on ours. But if we do begin to reflect and look deeper into our circumstances, dusting for the divine fingerprints present in any given situation, it will reveal two important things to us about the nature of God's work and presence in our lives. These truths set the stage for us to understand that there is, in fact, no such thing as "ordinary."

The Scope of God's Work

First of all, we see the great scope of God's work. The day before Saul would encounter Samuel on that road, God whispered in Samuel's ear. Look again at what God said to His prophet about this forthcoming encounter:

> "At this time tomorrow I will send you a man
> from the land of Benjamin. Anoint him ruler
> over My people Israel. He will save them from
> the hand of the Philistines because I have seen
> the affliction of My people, for their cry has
> come to Me." (1 Sam. 9:16)

Do you see it? God didn't say, "A good-looking, albeit oblivious young man will come into town tomorrow." No, He claimed divine orchestration of this moment: "I will send you a man . . ."

This encounter wasn't by chance; it wasn't an accident by any stretch of the imagination. God had been involved in Saul's life for days and weeks and months and years, though Saul had no idea. Consider the amazing scope of the work of God to engineer this encounter. Evidently, God was so intricately involved in Saul's life and circumstances that He knew the exact right moment for some careless servant in Kish's house to leave the donkey pen unlatched. Even further, He knew how to direct the steps of those wandering donkeys to make sure that Saul and his servant followed them, without finding them, to the base of the hill in Zuph.

The question isn't whether or not God is present and active; the question is just how aware we are of that presence and activity. Just because we consider the ordinary details of life to be small and insignificant, devoid of any real meaning, doesn't mean that they are. And it certainly doesn't mean that God is uninvolved. In all those dirty diapers, bill payments, e-mails, and daily commutes, God is there. He is intimately involved in the small, seemingly insignificant areas of our lives. This leads us to the second point.

God's Work through the Ordinary

God operates through, not in spite of, these seemingly ordinary circumstances. Unlike Saul, we have the benefit of knowing what's happening behind the scenes.

And isn't there part of you that wants to grab him by his big tall shoulders and shake him out of his stupor? "Would you forget about the stupid donkeys already? Don't you see that there is something bigger going on here?" Likewise, we might look at this story and see ourselves in Saul. We are living our lives chasing donkeys. Paying bills, going to work, parenting, going to church week after week—donkeys, donkeys, donkeys. So maybe what we need to do is break out of the monotony. Broaden our focus. Quit chasing the donkeys of life and realize there's something bigger going on around us.

Right?

Wrong.

In this story, the donkeys aren't a distraction from the work of God; the donkeys are the mechanism that God used to awaken Saul to something deeper. Something he wasn't previously aware of. Something more than ordinary. Let me put it another way.

What if the pathway to significance isn't around the donkeys we find ourselves chasing day in and day out? What if it's *through* them? What if those ordinary details of life are actually the mechanism by which we get to see and experience God and His redemptive plan in a living and vibrant way?

The Illusion of Ordinary

Unfortunately, most of us have bought into the illusion of the ordinary. We long for an escape from our regular lives—something to change our lives from what they currently are into lives with more excitement, adventure, and meaning. Millions of people every day go to great lengths to actualize this kind of dream.

Sometimes it turns out good. When people decide to move from spiritual mediocrity and into radical obedience, that's a good thing. They might sell all their stuff and move across the ocean. Or they might take on the challenge of fostering a houseful of children. Or they might decide to start a nonprofit. That's all good.

Sadly, though, that's not always the story. For every person who moves in good ways away from the ordinary, there are ten stories of those who move in the opposite direction. They are so terrified of the normal and ordinary in their work, marriages, finances, and parenting, that they flee into something—*anything*—that holds the promise of importance. Of significance. Of excitement. The result is an affair. Or an addiction to porn. Or a gambling debt. Or an abandonment of family. All because so many of us suffer from the same, crippling fear that I do—the fear of the ordinary.

But there is no such thing as ordinary when you are following an extraordinary God. "Ordinary" is a myth. The only reason we think of something as ordinary is because we fail to look for and then grasp the massive depth of the work and presence of God in our lives. In fact, as we look through Scripture, we find God not removing people from the ordinary, but instead transforming that ordinary into something wholly different. All of a sudden His people wake up to His presence and purpose that have been there all the time.

It's true, we also find the miraculous, but more times than not, the miraculous is couched in a situation that to the people involved in it, would have been considered just a part of another day. Very boring. Boring, that is, until they began to more fully grasp the scope, power, and wisdom of God.

If indeed that's true—that there is no such thing as ordinary—then we need to rethink the way we are approaching our everyday lives. We need to reconsider what the pathway to significance looks like. And we need to rediscover a God who doesn't call us out of the ordinary, but transforms the ordinary by His very presence. It will change the way we pay our bills, go to work, parent our children, and have ordinary conversations.

Everything will start to have meaning. *Everything*.

So again I ask: What if a life of significance isn't found apart from the donkeys, but right in the middle of them? What if there is a way to live a normal, ordinary life in an extraordinary way? What if there is a way to keep one eye on the donkeys and one eye on the God who opened the pen?

I think there is.

CHAPTER 2

BELOW THE SURFACE

Cicada Invasion

The scene looked like a B-Horror movie from the 1960s. The landscape was dotted with holes from something subterranean that had emerged from below. The walls of homes were covered with moving creatures by the hundreds. Their dead excess skin coated the ground as thickly as a layer of mulch to the point that there was a distinct crackling sound as you moved cautiously through the grass.

That was the situation at my house in Nashville, Tennessee, in the summer of 2011—the year that would be known, at least in our family, as the invasion of the cicadas.

For ten weeks, the entire city had cicada fever. As I drove down the highway, it was like someone was pelting my windshield with jelly-filled donut holes as the hordes of insects strayed from the safety of the trees into oncoming traffic. Everywhere I went there was the constant buzzing in the air that sounded somewhere between a chain saw and the emergency broadcasting system warning. Restaurants tried their hand at insect delicacies, covering the invaders with chocolate or baking them into enchiladas. T-shirts and bumper stickers were sold. Umbrellas were employed against dive-bombing attacks. Children ran from school to the car to avoid the swarms. Other children collected cicadas by the hundreds and littered their front porches with Tupperware containers.

My five-year-old daughter was horrified at the entire spectacle, so I will never be the one to tell her the terrifying truth that the cicadas didn't migrate from somewhere else to Nashville. *They were already here.* Put that on a movie poster and you're guaranteed to sell tickets.

The cicada has a thirteen-year gestation period. For over a decade, the cicada eggs stay underground. Then, for whatever reason, something in their internal cuckoo clock goes off, the eggs hatch, and the little pests start to burrow out through the soil. Then, for several weeks, they sing (loudly), they mate, and then they die. During that time, they shed their skins too, so that when things finally quiet down, the yards of Nashville and other Southern cities look like there has been some sort of global insect apocalypse.

Carnage everywhere.

But before they end their gloriously loud and annoying little lives, fresh eggs are deposited in the ground. Once there, they wait and wait and wait. Thirteen years from now, we are going to see the kids of our little insect friends. The ones that have been there all the time, lurking below the surface.

Like I said, I'll never share this fact with my little girl. My boys would think it's awesome to know that millions of cicada eggs are a few inches deep in our yard right now, but my daughter would never go outside again. For me, the experience will forever change the way I walk across my lawn, for now I know that no matter how quiet things are on the surface, millions of cicadas are down there in the soil, out of eyesight, just waiting for the right moment to emerge. It's a little dizzying to think about, right? That you might be completely unaware of what's happening all around you? Completely oblivious that activity is teeming, just out of sight, all the while you are simply doing all the regular stuff of life. That's how it was for Saul.

Saul, engaged in the great donkey chase and crazy series of coincidences, had started off as a country boy looking for some runaway animals. Then, seemingly out of nowhere, he was being proclaimed as the first king of Israel. Quite a turn of events.

Perhaps Saul, in his more reflective moments, was at least a little bit amazed at how the whole thing had come about. He didn't accidentally blunder into this situation. The donkeys weren't mistakenly released, and he didn't just happen to find himself roaming around Zuph. The Lord was at work in unseen ways, below the surface, just waiting for the right time to reveal, at least in part, what He had been up to.

In our more reflective moments, surely we would acknowledge the same thing. That God is constantly at work, regardless of whether we recognize it or not. Or at least we would claim to acknowledge the same thing.

The Active (or Passive) God

If you're a Christian as I am, then you probably would acknowledge a belief in the pervasive and all-encompassing work of God. We would agree together that God is not passive but active, constantly moving and working in the world at all times. We say it, but do we really believe it? Or is it just a mantra we've picked up in evangelical circles?

I'm pretty sure that though we might assent to the idea that God is active, we are in reality practicing a kind of deism rather than true Christianity.

Deism has many of the same components as orthodox Christianity: a belief in a supreme being, an obligation to worship and to live ethically, a need for repentance from sins, and the promise of divine rewards after death. The key difference is in the way the deist believes God relates to the world.

The deist's understanding of the work of God has been classically likened to that of a clockmaker. God wound up the clock of the universe at the very beginning, and then took His hands off, letting things progress in their most natural way. The world now is running without the active involvement of God in world history until the time when the clock runs out and the world ends. In such a belief system, God's relationship to the world is reduced to being the first cause only.

"Ridiculous!" we might say. We don't believe such things . . . do we? Maybe not on paper. But I wonder if that religious system describes the way we function practically day in and day out, at least to an extent.

Think about it in terms of the way we pray.

One of the most common phrases that makes its way into our prayers is this: "Please be with so-and-so." I've said it. You've probably said it too. I know what we mean when we say this. Our friend or relative or whoever is going through a difficult circumstance. Maybe it's a life-threatening illness, or perhaps a particularly challenging set of final exams. Whatever the circumstances, we pray for that person during this time, and what we are really asking is for God to let them know that they are not alone. That He is with them. That He would comfort them in their anxiety, stress, or sadness.

That's what we mean, but that's not what we say.

We say, "Please be with them," implying that He isn't.

Where has God been? Was He on a break? Vacation? Preoccupied with other stuff? But now that there is some need, we need Him here. Now. Urgently.

It might sound like mere semantics, but words matter. They're revelatory. Perhaps we're not as confident in the active nature of God as we think we are.

The same applies to our daily schedules. Our everyday, run-of-the-mill, schedules. During the course of our ordinary days, when are we conscious of the presence of God? When we're eating our cold cereal? Getting our coffee from the workroom at the office? Folding laundry? Disciplining the kids? Coaching baseball practice? When? If ever?

The point is that most of us operate, at least subconsciously, under the default assumption that God is *not* near to us. That He has to be invited into a situation. That He's not active unless we ask Him to be.

That is simply not true.

The question isn't whether or not God is actively with us; the question is just how aware we are of His presence.

We don't need to pray that God would "be with"

someone; He already is. We don't need to ask the Lord to come into our worship services; He's already there. We don't need to assume that when we come into a new workplace, city, or other environment, that God is not already busy. He is. And He has been for quite some time.

Jesus got at this point in a number of instances of His teaching ministry. One such moment occurred during His most famous of lectures—the Sermon on the Mount as recorded in Matthew 5.

Birds, Flowers, and the Activity of God

Sometimes we take a twenty-first-century version of North American Christianity and import it into the Bible. When we read about Jesus preaching in front of a large crowd, we don't really consider the implications of the setting. A sermon, for us, is about sitting in a pew or a chair or maybe even on our couch with a set of earbuds in. The air conditioner or heater is running, and we are comfortable as we casually nod or take notes. We are well dressed and perhaps are even sipping a cup of the free coffee we got in the lobby.

You would have found a radically different setting on the day of Jesus' great sermon. The people would have been jammed together, either sitting on the ground or maybe even standing, for it was customary in those days for the teacher to sit and the audience to be on their feet. Probably not a whole lot of shade from the hot sun, either. What might have made it even more uncomfortable were the people in attendance.

If we look back at a couple of chapters in the Bible to Matthew 4, we get a good picture of the rabble that was following Jesus:

> Then the news about Him spread throughout Syria. So they brought to Him all those who were afflicted, those suffering from various diseases and intense pains, the demon-possessed, the epileptics, and the paralytics. And He healed them. Large crowds followed Him from Galilee, Decapolis, Jerusalem, Judea, and beyond the Jordan. (Matt. 4:24–25)

Jesus, even this early in His ministry, was developing quite a following. And a reputation. People were coming out of the woodwork, in large part because this man was healing the sick and associating with people no one else would. He spoke with authority and loved generously. What do we think, then, that the crowds looked like as they sat on the hill that day? Suits and ties? Sundresses?

There was no polite listening here. No nicely dressed parishioners with moleskin notebooks and coffee cups in hand. Imagine men and women, shunned by society because of their physical ailments. Their sin. Their injuries. Their reputations. Horrible issues of illnesses of all kinds. Imagine the words of Jesus being interrupted by an epileptic seizure. Imagine the shrieks of the demon-possessed. While you're at it, consider the smell. Rotting flesh. Clothes dug out of garbage heaps. The scent, almost palpable, of people who have been discarded as unimportant and unnecessary and unclean by society.

These are the most regular of regular kinds of people. But Jesus? He looks at the crowd and smiles, for these are the people, so neglected and unloved, who are also so ready to hear the good news. So He begins to teach them, never once holding His nose.

Jesus taught them about the nature of the kingdom of God, how in this kingdom, everything is flipped on its head. Up is down. Left is right. Poor is rich. Hungry is full. Persecuted is blessed. He taught about how these people—the *ordinary* people—are salt and light to the rest of the world when they believe in Him. He taught them that their skin conditions and palsies and injuries and poverty were not the measure of their righteousness or purity. He taught them how dramatically different they become when they live in light of the great love of God. And on that subject of God's love, care, and provision, He encouraged them with the presence and active nature of His Father:

> "This is why I tell you: Don't worry about your
> life, what you will eat or what you will drink;
> or about your body, what you will wear. Isn't

life more than food and the body more than
clothing? Look at the birds of the sky: They
don't sow or reap or gather into barns, yet
your heavenly Father feeds them. Aren't you
worth more than they? Can any of you add a
single cubit to his height by worrying? And
why do you worry about clothes? Learn how
the wildflowers of the field grow: they don't
labor or spin thread. Yet I tell you that not
even Solomon in all his splendor was adorned
like one of these! If that's how God clothes
the grass of the field, which is here today and
thrown into the furnace tomorrow, won't He
do much more for you—you of little faith? So
don't worry, saying, 'What will we eat?' or
'What will we drink?' or 'What will we wear?'
For the idolaters eagerly seek all these things,
and your heavenly Father knows that you need
them. But seek first the kingdom of God and
His righteousness, and all these things will be
provided for you. Therefore don't worry about
tomorrow, because tomorrow will worry about
itself. Each day has enough trouble of its own."
(Matt. 6:25–34)

These were people who didn't know where their
next meal, shirt, or shekel would come from. Yet Jesus
assured them that there was no reason to worry. And
why not?

Because God is not some kind of cosmic clockmaker who set the world in motion and then withdrew, letting everything run its course. On the contrary—even the most basic, elemental parts of nature reveal just how involved God is in the ordinary.

"Look at the birds of the sky," Jesus says. "Those birds? They don't worry about having a fully vested 401K or a completely secure bank account. God is involved, feeding them with what they need. And what about the flowers? They look pretty good. Beautiful even. They look that way because God Himself clothes them."

Food. Clothes. Money. These are all important things, but they're also . . . well . . . boring. Ordinary. Vanilla. That's precisely the point.

Jesus tells us that we have no reason to worry, because if God is so active in providing for these parts of His world, how much more will He be actively involved in the seemingly menial, insignificant details of the crown jewel of His creation—you and me?

Once again, the question is not whether or not God is with us; the question is just how aware we are of His presence with us. Let's not stop there, because the news about the activity of God gets even better.

Three-Letter Words

There are some great three-letter words in the Bible. Take, for example, the word "but." It's used often in Scripture as a transition kind of word that lets you know that one thing might have been the true and final word, but then the situation changed. It's a very important word when it's applied to the state of mankind. Think about how Paul described the state of humanity in Ephesians 2. Ours was a pretty hopeless situation, filled with words and phrases like "dead in your trespasses and sins"; "disobedient"; "by nature children under wrath." Not much good news there.

Then comes that three-letter word, in this case, coupled with another three-letter word:

"But God . . ."

We were dead, but God . . .

We were children of wrath, but God . . .

We were without hope, but God . . .

God intervened in our situation, and He made everything new. We who were spiritually dead became alive. We who were children of wrath became heirs to the kingdom. We who were without hope received hope eternal. All this because of Jesus and His death and resurrection. That three-letter word, "but", informs a couple of other three-letter words that make the good news of God's activity even better—"for" and "all."

God Is For Us

You could say that God is *with* us. He certainly is. His presence abides with believers in the form of the

Holy Spirit. In a very literal sense, God makes His home inside of every Christian, for our bodies are the new temples. He is with us. Always. Even to the ends of the earth. But in the gospel, this truth is compounded to the nth degree. God is not only *with* us; God is *for* us. And that makes a huge difference.

Think about how many people you are "with" every-day. Coworkers. People at the grocery store. Those waiting to pump gas. Neighbors. Friends. You are with all these people. But are you *for* them?

With is a description of location; *for* is a description of action. *With* is about proximity. *For* is about advocacy. To be *for* another means to not only wish their good, but to actively employ all means possible to bring about their good. You are their proponent. Their defender. Their champion.

This is who God becomes for us in Christ: "What then are we to say about these things? If God is *for* us, who is against us?" (Rom. 8:31, emphasis added).

But wait . . . how do we know that God is for us? The answer is equally simple and profound: the cross of Jesus Christ: "He did not even spare His own Son but offered Him up for us all; how will He not also along with Him grant us everything?" (Rom. 8:32).

God could have abandoned humanity long ago, and been completely justified in doing so. We, by both our choices and our nature, are rebels against His loving care. His provision. His ways. We demonstrate day in and day out that we believe we are the better charters of our own destinies; that we are more good and wise than God Himself.

But He didn't abandon us.

The cross is the ultimate and final answer to the question of God's advocacy. He has proven His "forness" at Calvary.

What an astounding truth that is. God—God— Creator, Sustainer, and Author of life, is for us. For me. For you. In Christ.

But what does that really mean? Does it mean we're destined for wealth? Fame? Power? Hardly. Ironically, just a few verses after Paul drops the "for" bomb on us in Romans 8, he makes a pretty extensive list of things that we might think would separate us from God. These are bad things—cringe-worthy even: affliction; anguish; persecution; famine; nakedness; sword. Yikes. Now why would he include this list if these weren't real possibilities for the Christian? History rings with stories of believers in Jesus—those whom God is for—who have endured all such things. And worse.

God's advocacy does not mean we won't experience pain and hardship of the worst kind. To think it does is a drastic misinterpretation of the gospel. While there is no promise for a pain and trouble-free life, the fact that God is for us means, among other things, that in any circumstance, no matter how distressing or difficult, that we can know God is somehow working it for our good.

"We know that all things work together for the good of those who love God: those who are called according to His purpose" (Rom. 8:28). That's arguably one of the most quoted verses in the Bible—the stuff that sympathy cards are made of. But let's not mistake the word "good" here for the word "comfort." God does not work all things for the comfort of His people; He works all things for their good. That they might know Him in a deeper and more full way. That they would be conformed, little by little, into taking on the character of Jesus. And that they might learn the true value of the kingdom and King and help others see the same. God is actively—all the time—working things for our *good*.

Couched in that promise is the next three-letter word that deserves some extra attention: "all."

"ALL"

The way we read this word betrays our obsession with the big and important. When we read that God works all things together for our good, we tend to think of the most significant, life-altering situations we've ever experienced. We think of the cancer. The job loss. The death. The difficult relationships that go on for years. On the good side, we think about His miraculous provision during times of need. The healing. The wonderful friendship of another. The child. We take stock and look back over the course of our lives and realize that, in both the best and worst of times, God has been working for our good, even (and perhaps most especially) when we could not, for the life of us, perceive how.

But those are all big things. Curious, though, that the verse doesn't say that God works the big events of life for our good. Just as God goes beyond being with us to being for us, so He does not limit His work for our good to the big things. "All" is, if I could say it like this, much bigger than just the big things.

All means all.

It means the daily commute. The casual conversation over coffee. The date night with your spouse. The almost nightly discipline of your children. The prayer before dinner and the bedtime stories at night.

All means all.

"All" even goes beyond those events of which we are immediately aware. It means those things right now happening halfway across the world we have no idea about. It means political decisions made at the highest levels. It means acts of nature and random news stories we read about. Somehow, even these things are for our good. Such is the amazingly intricate work of God—that God might be working in yet unknown ways and in yet unknown people to provide for His people in yet unknown ways.

I know this from firsthand experience.

When my two-year-old son was diagnosed with leukemia, everything my wife and I thought we knew about God and life was brought into stark question. We didn't know what we needed, for it felt like the foundations of life were crumbling to the ground. Imagine how surprising it is now to look back and see that what we needed more than anything else was to be reminded of the gospel, over and over again.

And how did that happen? It happened not through an angelic visitation. It happened not through a message written in the stars. It happened because week in and week out we went to church and sat under the teaching of our pastor. And that happened because our pastor, Scott, had planted our church some twenty years earlier in Nashville. And that happened because he had agonized, those twenty years earlier while in seminary, about whether to return to ministry in his hometown of Nashville or stay in St. Louis where he had been in school.

One time, I heard Scott recount the story of those decision-making days. He went out into the woods one day and told God that he wasn't going anywhere until the Lord gave him some clear direction. Then after several hours he got hungry and went home without seeing a message written in the sky or finding a bush on fire but not burning up.

He eventually took a chance and started Grace Community Church. And twenty years later, a couple trying desperately to hang onto hope and faith came straggling into the back doors. I believe God had our family in mind when He positioned Scott in Nashville to launch this church where I now serve as an elder. Of course, we aren't the only people God had in mind. I hope I'm not arrogant enough to think we are. But that's really the point, isn't it? God somehow works for the good of millions of His children all at the same time through events they have no idea are going on.

See how staggering "all" is? It's unfathomable.

Broadening Your Vision

In the case of Saul, he couldn't seem to get a handle on the location of those donkeys. They were like wraiths, completely unfindable. And that's just how God wanted them to be. I'm sure more than once Saul threw up his hands in frustration. He even wanted to give up the search after a few days but only continued at the urging of his servant. For Saul, the chase was utterly meaningless. Just something to get through. He only after the fact possibly became aware of God's presence and work inside those days of frustratingly ordinary activity.

God was at work regardless of whether Saul recognized it. He's still doing the same thing, in ways we cannot possibly begin to comprehend. The work of God is not constrained to the big and audacious. His divine fingers steadily weave together the tapestry of the mundane and ordinary too. But for us, if we are indeed children of God in Christ, we have a different sort of confidence that someone like Saul could only imagine.

If Saul were able to zoom out and see the enormity of what was going on, he probably wouldn't have liked it very much. Imagine a series of concentric circles that represent Saul's scope of understanding. In Saul's limited vision, he was chasing donkeys. But if he were able to see one circle beyond, he'd have seen that the donkeys were leading him to a position of national importance. And if he could see another circle beyond that, he would have known that he was going to serve a different kind of purpose in God's plan than he expected.

Back in 1 Samuel 9, it's telling to note that God never once refers to Saul using regal language. He's referred to as "ruler" but not king. Interesting, right? Perhaps here we see that God was not giving up His own claim to the throne. Sure, Saul might be the temporary ruler, but ultimately God is king. Saul's reign would have its highs and lows, but it would end in disastrous fashion and pave the way for the great king David.

Let's go another circle beyond that, and we see that David, though he was a great king and described as a man after God's own heart, only served as a model of the greatest King. David was only a foreshadowing of the true monarch and champion for the people of God: Jesus Christ.

We are not like Saul. We are not destined to fail but to reign. We are coheirs with Jesus, and that is an inheritance that's never, ever going to be taken away. It's been sealed with the promise of the Holy Spirit in our lives. So when we begin to enlarge our own vision—to see beyond the mere physical and embrace the presence and work of God in all spheres of life at all times—we can do so with great confidence and faith.

We find ourselves bored in life not because of the absence of the extraordinary but because of our paralyzing lack of vision. We, as G. K. Chesterton put it, are "perishing for want of wonder, not want of wonders." But it doesn't have to be this way. Not if you believe in a God who is extraordinary enough to fill the ordinary. In fact, when we begin to see God and His work and presence with this perspective, it means we can do something that never entered the mind of Saul: We can chase the donkeys of life in faith, for faith is the avenue by which we can see the extraordinary in the midst of the ordinary.

We can pay the bills, go to the job, play with the kids, change the diapers, and whatever ordinary boring details real life involves, but we can do so in faith. We can actually begin to believe that what we are doing has significance and purpose. We can believe in the great and intricate plan of God, embracing His "forness" and the extent of "all" and believe that the donkeys matter. They have significance.

And so do we.

CHAPTER 3

THE DIVINE INVASION

Think, for a minute, about a fast-food restaurant in your community. It doesn't matter if you get tacos, burgers, salads, or some concoction in between. Think about the establishment—the actual brick-and-mortar store. Now think about what's around it. Chances are you could stand in the parking lot of that Burger King and throw a rock and hit McDonald's. Or you could put one hand on the side of a Taco Bell and run to a Wendy's in less than three seconds. You have, in a single square mile, countless eating establishments, all of which are only slight variations of each other.

It seems counterintuitive, doesn't it? How could a McDonald's possibly service right next to a Burger King? How could a Subway make money so close to a Jersey Mike's? It doesn't make sense. Unless, of course, you begin to embrace the one thing that drives these restaurants and other businesses. They know something about us that gives them the confidence to set up shop right next to their competitors: We are consumers. All of us. And consumers like options. We like options in the sense that we don't want to have the same sandwich every night. We like to vary our diets between equally unhealthy choices. But that's not the only reason we like options. We value options because we value escape.

Consumers like to escape. We like to know that even though we might badly want a gordita, we can move over and get a spicy Italian sub if the line is too long. We like to know that we aren't backed into a corner and can simply cut across the street if something about our first experience isn't to our liking.

As consumers, we see this as our sovereign right—to simply move on when some product doesn't meet our exact specifications. To escape any given situation that meet our standards, when something isn't exciting or fulfilling enough, or when something isn't comfortable.

Just like we run from one burger joint to another to find something that better suits us, we are daily seeking to escape from the routines of marriage, parenting, work, and church. But if what we've been saying in this book is true, the answer to the boredom we feel isn't escape. It's not to exercise what we believe to be our right as consumers of life. The answer is instead to rebel against the consumeristic tendencies inside of us. It's to stay, though everything in us might be screaming for us to leave. The answer is to find the meaning hiding behind the boring, everyday details of life.

The Uncommon Common

God's constant presence is ultimately what makes the insignificant become significant. If we look through the pages of Scripture, we find time and time again God invading the ordinary and then making the ordinary into something extraordinary. It's not that the thing itself changes; rather, whatever it is, in the midst of its ordinariness, becomes extraordinary by the virtue of the presence of God.

Jacob, when he was fleeing from the wrath of his big brother, slept on a regular old rock and had a dream of a ladder going up to heaven. He woke up and realized He was in the presence of the Lord, and that regular rock he used for a pillow became an enduring altar given to the worship of the Lord.

Moses, after spending forty years in utter obscurity and commonality as a shepherd, one day came upon a bush. It was a bush like you might see on any other hill on any other day except this ordinary bush was infused with something extraordinary—a fire that engulfed it and yet did not cause it to burn up. Moses took off his shoes in the presence of the extraordinary God.

Then God told him he would be the great deliverer the enslaved people of Israel had been praying for over the last four centuries. The instrument of that deliverance—the thing Moses would use to demonstrate the power of God—was to be a common, ordinary, shepherd's staff.

When the prophet Elijah, during a moment of great depression, was told to go and stand on the mountain and wait for the Lord's presence, God was not found in the mighty, loud, and majestic. Instead, the presence of the Lord came in a soft whisper.

When the Lord wanted to deliver a powerful message to His people about the nature of their covenant and the enduring love He felt for them during the days of the prophet Hosea, He did not choose to communicate it using a message in the sky. Instead, He used an ordinary marriage, complete with all the marital problems you might imagine (plus a few more that I hope you can't), to demonstrate His extraordinary commitment to His people.

The pattern continues as you flip to the New Testament. Who could imagine something more uncommon, something more extraordinary than God Himself coming to Earth as a man? The incarnation is astounding, and yet this baby was born into a back-water town whose only mark of significance was an obscure, centuries-old prophecy. He was born to common parents—a regular girl with a regular husband who had a regular job and no hope of ever changing his station in life. His birth was witnessed by plain old farm animals and the members of society on the lowest rung of the class totem pole. And His name? Well, that was as vanilla as they come.

Jesus is the Hebrew equivalent of being named "Joe." There were probably four other kids in His class with the same name. Nothing special there. But that's how God works.

He takes the common, and by His very presence, changes it into the uncommon. The regular becomes amazing. The ordinary becomes marvelous.

When this regular man, who was not extraordinarily handsome, tall, short, fat or thin, but had no beauty of majesty to attract anyone to Him began His ministry, He constantly took the common and made it something different.

The water.

The loaves.

The fish.

The mud.

All regular, everyday parts of life until they came into contact with the presence of Jesus. But why stop there? He's still doing the same thing.

Who did Jesus entrust with His divine mission? With the extraordinary message of the gospel? The most radically ordinary people imaginable. Twelve regular guys who were not particularly educated or articulate. And we, the regular people of today, follow in their footsteps. There's nothing extraordinary about us. We are the very definition of the word *ordinary*.

Or at least we were. But now, because of Jesus, once again the ordinary has been infused with the extraordinary. And now we, like the bush and the staff, like the loaves and the fish, have ceased to be mundane. Regular. Ordinary.

We've become something different, and no area of our lives is untouched. Because Jesus is here, now, there is no such thing as ordinary any more.

It sounds simple, doesn't it? Jesus has and is still making the ordinary extraordinary, not by transforming it as much as He is transforming us and the manner in which we see all things. But it's one thing to intellectually recognize all this. We can easily say, with gusto even, "Yes! There is no such thing as ordinary!" but as soon as we say it, we will be confronted with an endless progression of the mundane. What changes isn't so much the obligations and responsibilities of everyday life; those keep on coming as surely as the sun will rise tomorrow. What changes is the perspective with which we see those things. The poet Elizabeth Browning once mused that "earth is crammed with heaven and every common bush afire with God, but only he who sees takes off his shoes, the rest sit around and pick blackberries." We can, through Christ, begin to see the extraordinary God not in spite of our ordinary lives, not by escaping the monotony, but right in the middle of it. We can, to use Browning's words, take off our shoes when we see the divine invasion all around us. But this perspective change isn't something that suddenly comes upon us. Instead, it's something that must be actively sought out and even fought for.

The Necessity of Contentment

In his classic work *Orthodoxy*, G. K. Chesterton reflected on what we might learn about the extraordinary monotony of God from the excitement of our kids:

A child kicks his legs rhythmically through excess, not absence, of life. Because children have abounding vitality, because they are in spirit fierce and free, therefore they want things repeated and unchanged. They always say, "Do it again"; and the grown-up person does it again until he is nearly dead. For grown-up people are not strong enough to exult in monotony. But perhaps God is strong enough to exult in monotony. It is possible that God says every morning, "Do it again" to the sun; and every evening, "Do it again" to

the moon. It may not be automatic necessity
that makes all daisies alike; it may be that God
makes every daisy separately, but has never
got tired of making them. It may be that He
has the eternal appetite of infancy; for we
have sinned and grown old, and our Father is
younger than we.[1]

According to Chesterton, it is a mark of strength, not weakness, to do the same thing again and again. It is, then, the weak man who is constantly searching and seeking out the next great thing, never content with what stands before him. Ironically, it is the ability to do that which we might consider mundane with honor and even joy that is most difficult for us. We must, in a sense, *fight to not fight* to escape the ordinary. When we do, we'll find the extraordinary lurking inside what has become ordinary to us.

With what do we wage this battle? How do we actively engage? It is by developing a characteristic that is drastically more important to God than it is to us. It is a trait that is sometimes painted, even in Christian circles, as a lack of vision and initiative, and yet one that is essential if we really want to see the myth of the ordinary exposed. The trait in question is that of contentment.

The person of contentment isn't constantly striving after something else. He rebels against a culture of consumers who are maxing out their lives along with the credit cards because they've believed the marketing lie espoused by everything from sex to a bigger TV: "You deserve this." The content man stands against this falsehood.

He knows he has enough. Surely such an attitude is a great honor to God and essential for living in the middle of the ordinary. But because of the cultural emphases on more (not to mention our own sinfulness that constantly pushes our hearts toward excess), finding contentment is an exceedingly difficult proposition. Maybe even impossible.

Is it any wonder, then, that contentment is specifically what Paul referenced in the well-worn verse of Philippians 4:13: "I can do all things through Christ who strengthens me."

I had that verse written on a little slip of paper that I kept inside my football locker when I was in high school. "I can do all things through Christ who strengthens me," meaning that I could knock some guy on his can because Jesus was on my team. I guess I assumed there couldn't possibly be any dedicated Christians on the other team who might have written the same verse on their own lockers.

Too bad that verse isn't talking about football. Paul isn't talking about triumphalism, the idea that if we only believe, all our plans are going to succeed through Christ. Philippians 4:13 is about contentment. The context reveals that the specific thing Paul could do through Christ's strength was "learn the secret of being content in any and every situation" (v. 12 NIV). Evidently, contentment is so difficult a characteristic to develop and maintain that it can only be exercised in and through the strength of Christ.

It is important to note that contentment might not look exactly like we think it does. When I think of contentment, I think of someone like Bob Cratchett in Dickens' *A Christmas Carol*, who had next to nothing and a ton of mouths to feed with it. And yet his family was content with what they had—filled with thankfulness even when they weren't filled with turkey.

That's usually how we think about this characteristic. It's about choosing to have only two shirts in your closet, living on 10 percent of your income, and eating nothing but bread and bologna. Contentment, in our minds, is about training ourselves to settle for less.

No doubt that's part of it. When we indulge ourselves in everything the world has to offer simply because we can, we aren't making ourselves more content by getting more stuff; we're actually feeding the insatiable beast inside us that will always crave more and more and more.

True contentment isn't about settling for less. It's about seeing the true value of what we already do have in Christ. In his letter to the Ephesians, Paul would write about our wealth in Christ like this:

Praise be to the God and Father of our Lord Jesus Christ, who has blessed us in the heavenly realms with every spiritual blessing in Christ. For he chose us in him before the creation of the world to be holy and blameless in his sight. In love he predestined us to be adopted as his sons through Jesus Christ, in accordance with his pleasure and will—to the praise of his glorious grace, which he has freely given us in the One he loves. In him we have redemption through his blood, the forgiveness of sins, in accordance with the riches of God's grace that he lavished on us with all wisdom and understanding. And he made known to us the mystery of his will according to his good pleasure, which he purposed in Christ, to be put into effect when the times will have reached their fulfillment—to bring all things in heaven and on earth together under one head, even Christ. (Eph. 1:3–10 NIV)

He goes on to further enumerate these spiritual blessings until our heads are left ringing with the depth of our riches in Christ. We, like Scrooge McDuck, are swimming in a money bin full of adoption, lavished grace, understanding, and redemption. But here again we find the old enemy of God and mankind spinning lies about the nature of God with the purpose of keeping us from understanding the fullness of what's been

51

given to us in Christ. If we're not careful, we might look around us and be fooled into thinking that God is holding out on us.

God Is Not a Miser

You can see how we might think that God is holding out on us, right? It's the age-old question of the problem of human pain. When the job loss, the cancer, the breakup, or whatever comes into our lives, often the first question comes as a charge against God: "How could You let this happen? Don't You love me? Because if You did, my circumstances wouldn't look like this."

This issue is as old at the entrance of sin into the world. We have a natural tendency to evaluate God's blessing and opinion of us based on our circumstances. But the ultimate measure of God's love is not our health, wealth, and prosperity: It's the cross. That's how we know God loves us.

Even given that, there is still something inside of us, even as Christians, that looks for something more. Something secondary. Something more exciting from God. We say we want to "go deeper," when what we really mean is that we want to feel more. So we search for religious experience after religious experience, each time hoping that we will be moved to some greater level of emotional impact, feeling God in some new and fresh way. But can I tell you something?

Something that might just free you from that endless search of something else from God? Something that might keep you from going down to the altar again and again to rededicate your life . . . again?

God is not a miser. He's not holding out on us. There isn't anything else if you have been given Jesus. We know that God has held nothing back from us in Christ, for if He gave up His Son for us, how would He not also, along with Him, graciously give us all things (Rom. 8:32)? And we know that in the gospel, God has already given the Christian every spiritual blessing in Christ (Eph. 1:3). He's given us everything He has to give in Christ. In fact, the very idea that there might be something else is a direct challenge to the love of God, and ultimately the subtext behind Satan's words in the garden in Genesis 3.

At first, we might read the temptation to Eve as pretty straightforward and simple: "Did God really say that you can't eat from any tree in the garden?" It's a twisting of God's Word, to be sure. He had told His children that they could eat from any tree in the garden, save one. But the serpent—the cunning serpent—caused Eve to focus on the prohibition rather than the freedom. He moved her to focus on the negative—what she could not have—as opposed to the hundreds or even thousands of trees she could. If we read between the lines, we can imagine the message behind Satan's words going something like this:

God is not generous toward you. He doesn't really love you. If He did, He wouldn't be holding out on you. He doesn't want you to be happy, and the way you know it is because there's something else out there that He won't let you have.

So destructive. So insidious. So subversive. It wasn't just a piece of fruit at stake here; the real issue was whether or not these first humans really trusted that God loved them, knew what was best for them, and was lovingly generous toward them. Discontentment is a vicarious charge against the sufficiency and goodness of God. Eve was tricked into thinking that there was indeed something else; her discontentment was aroused and we know the rest of the story.

On the flip side, when we are content—not because we've learned to settle for less, but because we are undone by how much we've been given in Christ—we are living testaments to the love and generosity of God. Understanding what we have in Christ is the beginning of the fight against the constant desire for something else, whether that "else" is money, or power, or excitement. When we live in such a state of gratitude, we are poised to see the extraordinary God in the midst of the ordinary. We must fight for this, through Christ who strengthens us, by praying for and pursuing an ever-growing understanding of the riches of the gospel. When we become convinced that God, in His grace, has held nothing back from us in Christ, then we can stop our wandering eyes and hearts from continually seeking out something else. Something more. Something further. We can instead be freed to live in the middle of the great riches of Jesus. And when we do, we'll realize more and more that the extraordinary has come. He was born. He lived a perfect life and died a sinner's death. And we have been made new in Him. We are the sons and daughters of God. Adopted children. And for people like that, who know who they are and what they already have, they don't need anything else.

Breaking Down Partitions

For the Christian, all of life—all the ordinary, mundane moments—are infused with the presence and work of an extraordinary God. That means that escape from the ordinary is actually found not so much by neglecting the seemingly unimportant, but by seeing the meaning of the ordinary in light of the presence of Jesus.

As a result, we must actively seek to break down the walls between those parts of life we typically see as exciting and, well, everything else:

> For though we live in the body, we do not wage
> war in an unspiritual way, since the weapons
> of our warfare are not worldly, but are power-
> ful through God for the demolition of strong-
> holds. We demolish arguments and every

high-minded thing that is raised up against the knowledge of God, taking every thought captive to obey Christ. (2 Cor. 10:3–5)

What Paul calls the "high-minded things" in this passage are literally *partitions*. They are walls that separate the sacred from the secular, the special from the mundane. It is His intent that we wage spiritual war on these things, for they are raised up against the knowledge of God. The end result is that we take captive every thought—not just the exciting ones, but the boring ones as well, and bring them in line with Jesus. That means we wage war on thoughts of lust and power, but it also means we wage war on thoughts of boredom and insignificance. We, through the power of God, begin to see that every area of life is filled, through the presence of God, with tremendous meaning and significance. The high-minded things come tumbling down.

It's one thing to say this from an intellectual standpoint; it's another thing to actually bring a greater sense of awareness of God's extraordinary activity to the common areas of everyday life. That's what the rest of this book is about. The remaining chapters focus on a few key aspects of life that, if we're not careful, can slip into the rut of monotony: discipleship, friendships, marriage, parenting, money, work, and church. My hope, as you read, is that these seemingly ordinary areas of life start to become extraordinary as we break down those partitions that separate the boring from the amazing.

My prayer is that paying taxes would no longer be just about paying taxes. Changing diapers would be about something more. Disciplining your kids and loving your spouse would become extraordinary. Going to work would transform into something about far more than earning a paycheck. When we view the ordinary areas of life through the lens of the Holy Spirit, we begin to understand that there is really no such thing as ordinary. Then we can become, more and more, like the children Chesterton described. Instead of pining away, day after day, searching for something else, we will look in wonder at the whole of life and say to the Lord, "Do it again."

CHAPTER 4

EARLY TO BED, EARLY TO RISE

The college I attended had an interesting dynamic. Though I was at a small, secular university—a state school in the panhandle of Texas—the number of Christians drastically outnumbered the number of non-Christians. And these weren't just any old Christians. These were the people who spent summers overseas serving others for the sake of the gospel. This was an environment where David Crowder and Chris Tomlin were as popular as Bono or Pearl Jam, and approximately one-third of the student body gathered together every Thursday night for a two-hour worship experience.

It was pretty amazing. I will admit, though, that much of the time I cut out a little early since worship didn't begin until 10 p.m.

My dad was a statistics professor at this university as he had been for the previous fifteen years. There were a lot of days, particularly Fridays, when I would straggle into his office after an 8 a.m. class, unshaven and tired, and talk about how great worship was the previous night. Dad would smile and nod, ask a few questions here and there, and be genuinely excited about what the Lord was doing on campus.

One particular morning has stuck with me over the years. During one of these visits, my dad wondered aloud, almost to himself, about the attendance of some of the folks involved in that worship service to his classes on Friday morning. He noted a significant drop off of the Christian leaders on campus on Fridays, so he mused: "You know, son, sometimes the most spiritual thing you can do is go to bed early and show up to class on time."

I laughed it off at the time with the arrogance that only a freshman in college can have. And yet . . .

And yet there's something there, isn't there? Does attendance at a worship service justify the missing of class? What does it say to professors when their students flunk quizzes because they were so busy studying the

Bible that they didn't have time to pick up their text-books? Is God pleased by that kind of behavior?

It's a valid question, one that I still don't have an answer to, but I would venture to say the fact that we ask such a question points out a misshapen idea of what God really wants from us in life. Long before we ask any of the more exciting questions about what vocation to choose, what person to marry, or what city to live in, we should be asking: What does God really want from all of us?

Disciples

It might sound boring, but at a fundamental level, God wants the exact same thing from you and me as He has wanted from every other person who names the name of Jesus as Lord: He wants us to truly fol-low Jesus. To be His disciples. That was, after all, the marching orders Jesus left for His church: "Go, there-fore, and make disciples of all nations . . ." (Matt. 28:19).

The problem is that *disciple* is one of those words in the Christian vocabulary that has been so often used, so often quoted, that we've lost a bit of its meaning. If this is what God ultimately wants from us, then that definition should be incredibly meaningful. We should be mining it for all it's worth, trying in an ever-increas-ing way to understand it more fully. So what, then, does it mean to be a disciple of Jesus?

Literally, the word means "to follow." Disciples of Jesus are followers of Jesus. They walk not only where He walks, but in the manner in which He walks. It means that we acknowledge the lordship of Jesus and seek to see that lordship actualized in every area of our lives. That's what disciples do.

Drop Your Nets

Jesus' first call to discipleship in Scripture gives us a good picture of how a disciple responds to Him:

> As He was passing along by the Sea of Galilee,
> He saw Simon and Andrew, Simon's brother.
> They were casting a net into the sea, since
> they were fishermen. "Follow Me," Jesus told
> them, "and I will make you fish for people!"
> Immediately they left their nets and followed
> Him. (Mark 1:16–18)

Notice particularly what happened in that passage. The call of Jesus went out, and the men dropped their nets. Now I'm sure there's a practical component to this—they dropped their nets because that's what they were holding at the time. You can't really walk off following some random rabbi with a bunch of fishing nets in your hands. Still, it does seem like a strange detail to include in the account. Mark didn't say, "They shielded their eyes from the sun" or "They took a step out of the boat."

They dropped their nets. They symbolically left their old way of life. They broke with the past—their past vocation, their sense of self, and their identity— and fully embraced the future. Those nets were the symbols of their livelihood—the very tools they would use to make their way in the world. And they dropped them and instead followed Jesus. That's what a disciple does.

Disciples recognize the worth and value of the One who calls and see the "nets" in their hands in comparison to Him. They suddenly realize that they have a greater purpose than merely fishing; so they leave and follow Jesus instead. For disciples, following Jesus is both an exit and an entrance; an ending as well as a beginning. They charge off, not knowing exactly what the future entails, but knowing that whatever it is they'll follow Jesus into it.

That's how all of us started our life with Christ. And it's a commitment that we renew day after day, moment by moment. Following Jesus is something that doesn't only require a piece of a person; it requires the whole of who we are and what we have. It's an all-the-time thing.

God the Discipler

God, for His part, engages in the lifelong process of conforming each of us to the likeness of His Son. We drop our nets, and the Holy Spirit begins to chip away at our long-held dreams, assumptions, desires, and ambitions, making us more and more like Jesus in the process. The disciple doesn't only follow Jesus; he becomes more like Jesus. This is what God has planned for you and me since before time began:

> For those He foreknew He also predestined to be conformed to the image of His Son, so that He would be the firstborn among many brothers. And those He predestined, He also called; and those He called, He also justified; and those He justified, He also glorified. (Rom. 8:29–30)

This is what God has thrown His weight behind. This is what He is doing in every Christian, regardless of how mundane or exciting you think your life is. This is, we can say, God's will for your life.

But here's the problem: That's not very exciting.

Is it?

How fired up do you really get about knowing that the thing God is doing in you is making you more like Jesus? If we're honest, most of us would rather hear that God is preparing a place of incredible influence for us. Or that God has some grand adventure in mind for us. Or that God has an exciting life of prosperity put out before us. Those things may or may not be true for you, but one thing certainly is: If you're a Christian, then God's will for your life is that you are being conformed to the likeness of Christ. Furthermore, God is only doing those other things in your future to the degree that they accomplish this fundamental purpose. If they do not, then He is not.

Slow and Steady

Most of the mechanisms God uses to transform us into Christlikeness aren't the big, but the small. They are the series of choices we face day after day. This is how Paul described growing in Christ—not as something exciting, but as a methodical process akin to that of athletic training:

> Don't you know that the runners in a stadium all race, but only one receives the prize? Run in such a way to win the prize. Now everyone who competes exercises self-control in everything. However, they do it to receive a crown that will fade away, but we a crown that will never fade away. Therefore I do not run like one who runs aimlessly or box like one beating the air. Instead, I discipline my body and bring it under strict control, so that after

preaching to others, I myself will not be disqualified. (1 Cor. 9:24–27)

Despite what the training montages in the *Rocky* movies might lead you to believe, being an athlete is hard work. It's not accomplished in five minutes and it's not usually done to the sound track of "The Eye of the Tiger." Staying in top shape requires waking up at 4 a.m. every morning and going to bed early every night; having a plan for what you eat and how you spend your time; making sure that all the small choices in life point to the one goal. That's the metaphor Paul chose for growing in Christ—it's an athletic contest, not a magic show where doves come flying out of a hat.

One of the reasons that everything has meaning for us as disciples of Christ is because everything is either moving us toward Christlikeness or away from it. Every choice isn't just about the choice—it's about whether we are embracing our sanctification or pushing against it. Paul knew the surpassing greatness of knowing Christ—that He is so valuable that anything stacked up against Him looks like dung. Is it any wonder, then, that he would, just one chapter after 1 Corinthians 9, also exhort those in Corinth to consider the little things of life as an opportunity to glorify God? "So whether you eat or drink or whatever you do, do it all for the glory of God" (1 Cor. 10:31 NIV).

These common, everyday choices are the guts of discipleship. Following Christ is not just about selling everything you have for the sake of the poor (though it might indeed be that at some point); it also involves managing your time; appropriately handling your throwaway thoughts; glorifying God through your eating and drinking; seeing the small things of life as things that either move you toward or away from Christlikeness. Disciples understand the true significance of these choices.

When was the last time you or I thought about these things? Chances are we haven't considered them nearly as often as God has. As much as we might long for something new and different, something more exciting and fresh, God is still vitally concerned that we make the everyday, run-of-the-mill choices of faithfulness because we desire the same thing that He does—to more and more resemble His Son.

Many of us, in an effort to spice things up a little bit, have abandoned thinking deeply about and struggling with these choices. Similarly, we have abandoned the everyday practices of saints of the past, looking for something a little bit more modern and progressive. So we find ourselves bowing down to the idol of excitement all while claiming to be seeking after the living God.

We don't need something new. We need something old. We need to do the same things that saints of old have been doing in order to deepen our understanding and apprehension of the greatness of God. We need to see that it's not some kind of secret formula or latest methodology that exposes the myth of the ordinary. Instead it's through these means of grace that many of us have cast aside as outdated and legalistic that God has chosen to deepen our relationship and experience with Him.

The Quiet Time and Other Boring Stuff

To put it practically, maybe it's time we actually start having a quiet time again. And not just that. Maybe we need to practice devoted prayer, memorize Scripture, and fast. Maybe we need to do all these things that are meant to characterize the life of the disciple.

Over time, these disciplines have fallen steadily out of favor in Christian practice. We have come to see them as outdated practices that bind people in legalistic pursuits, and have instead drifted toward more "spiritual" ways of communing with God. The impetus behind this drift more times than not involves "feelings." We don't feel God when it's just us and the Bible. We don't feel God when we try to pray. We want something bigger— something more emotive—an environment filled with smoke and lights and all kinds of atmospheric aids in which we can truly sense the presence of God.

But here is something we need to consider carefully before we abandon these "outdated" practices: What purpose do feelings really serve? More specifically, can our feelings really be trusted as an accurate gauge of the presence and blessing of God? I would argue that the answer is no.

Ideally, I would wake up every morning with a burning desire to read the Bible. I would jump—literally—out of bed with my mind salivating for time in the Word. But I don't. I hit the snooze button. Most days I straggle to the Bible still wiping the sleep from my eyes. I don't *feel* like reading the Bible at all—I *feel* like sleeping. But on the best days, I read anyway, because feelings follow faith.

Feelings follow faith. Not the other way around.

When we engage in these spiritual disciplines like prayer, Bible study, Scripture memory, fasting, and others of these little marks of faithfulness throughout daily life, we do so not because we feel like it, but because we believe that if we do, God will meet us in the middle of them. Our action is not fueled by what our finicky feelings might tell us to do one moment to the next, but instead by what we know to be true.

God has inspired His Word.

Purity is His plan.

He desires a life of faithfulness.

Faith is the engine of the train and feelings are the caboose that is pulled along.

Many of us find ourselves right now worshipping not at the altar of God but at the altar of excitement.

We bow down to what is most noteworthy of the day, as determined by our emotions, and we firmly plant our allegiance and obedience there. But that's not the picture God offers of the life of the disciple:

> The man who trusts in the LORD, whose confidence indeed is the LORD, is blessed. He will be like a tree planted by water: it sends its roots out toward a stream, it doesn't fear when heat comes, and its foliage remains green. It will not worry in a year of drought or cease producing fruit. (Jer. 17:7–8)

What an amazing picture. Notice, though, that this great tree of a man, the one who is solid and stable, doesn't get there due to his feelings but because of his faith. He trusts in the Lord. That's not to say he doesn't "feel" the Lord, but it is to say that such a man had made it his practice to drink deeply of the Lord regardless of the season. Heat or no heat. Feelings or no feelings. Psalm 1 offers a similar picture of a stable oak; in this passage, that stability is linked specifically to the fact that he delights in the law of the Lord:

> How happy is the man who does not follow the advice of the wicked or take the path of sinners or join a group of mockers! Instead, his delight is in the LORD's instruction, and he meditates on it day and night. He is like a tree planted beside streams of water that bears its

fruit in season and whose leaf does not wither.
Whatever he does prospers. (Ps. 1:1–3)

Put yourself in the place of the tree for a second.
I'm sure the tree is grateful for the rain when it comes.
I'm sure it feels nice to have your leaves pelted with
drops of precipitation and an abundance of water to
soak near the surface. But trees know (if indeed trees
could know) that the surface water is the exception
rather than the rule. It's not going to rain everyday.

The strong trees—the trees that last—put in the
hard work of growing deeper. They store up what
water they can, but their default mechanism is to keep
pushing. Down and down. Further and further. Day by
day. They do so because if they go deep enough, they'll
eventually hit the real water. Not the kind that comes
and goes, but the streams that run deep beneath the
surface and never run dry.

Faith leads to obedience. Feelings are pulled along
by that engine of faith. If we wait for the excitement, for
the feelings, then we'll be waiting a long time. And our
spiritual lives will not be characterized by the strength
and fortitude of deep roots. Rather than sturdy oaks
we will be more like yo-yos, constantly moving up and
down the string of life's circumstances driven by those
same feelings we long for.

Who do you want to be when the cancer comes?
When the job is lost? When the economy crashes? Do
you want to be the stable tree or the yo-yo? If it's the

former, then we must put down roots. We must engage in the time-tested practices of spiritual growth. And we must do in faith.

Sailboats

Perhaps one more example will help us to see the place of these boring disciplines in the life of the disciple of Jesus Christ. Think about it in terms of different kinds of boats.

Think first about a bass boat. You know, something with a powerful motor designed to get you from one end of the lake to the other as quickly as possible. The movement of something like a bass boat is passive. You turn the key, move the accelerator, and then hold on. It's true, there's no feeling like the wind whipping through your hair as you skim across the surface of the water. Sometimes life with Jesus feels like that—that He is moving and working in visible ways and the only thing you can do is hang on and pick the bugs out of your teeth.

Being in a rowboat is very different. There is no key. There is no accelerator. You know what there is instead? Arms. And oars. Movement in a rowboat is directly related to the strength of the one rowing. The distance you can go is dependent on the strength of your back. You don't go very fast, but movement is steady, and slowly you can make good progress if you're strong enough to keep on moving the oars. Sometimes life with Jesus feels like that too—that you are plodding along, one stroke at a time, not going very quickly and certainly not moving in an exciting way.

But for the disciple, a better picture of engaging the spiritual disciplines is that of a sailboat. It takes a lot of small choices to make the sailboat move. There are knots to be tied. There are sails to be raised. There are courses to be charted. So you do these small things, methodically, one at a time, and they're hard work. But ultimately, none of those things moves you. Movement in the sailboat is about the wind. All the other actions you take are only meant to position yourself in such a manner as to catch the wind. Such is the case with these disciplines.

You pray, you fast, you read and memorize Scripture day in and day out because you believe that if you do these things, the wind is going to eventually start blowing. You are putting your life in a position in which you can catch that wind of God and be taken for a ride. It's not very exciting on the front end, but once it happens, you see the result of all the mundanity and the boredom.

And by the way, the direct translation from the Greek words for Holy Spirit is "divine wind."

Are you worshipping at the altar of excitement? Do these practices seem outdated and boring to you?

Maybe you don't need something new. Maybe you need to see these practices through the lens of faith. And maybe, if you do, you'll find that the wind has been blowing all the time. You just needed to raise the sail.

CHAPTER 5

SHOOTING THE BREEZE

In March of 2006, a small but dedicated team began work on the social networking service that would become Twitter. The fledgling platform was ready for its first tweet on March 21, after only eight days of programming. As it turned out, it was a pretty good idea. In fact, at the time of this writing, Twitter users were approaching one billion, and the service has become one of the primary outlets through which news is disseminated.

That's one billion people communicating details about their hopes, dreams, fears, aspirations, and breakfast in 140 characters or less. Though when the service launched, we might have scoffed at the idea that others would be interested in knowing how cutely we can pose our pets or how delicious our hamburger looks. We were apparently wrong. Then again, we shouldn't have been surprised because Twitter is the natural next step in the progression of human relationships.

Once upon a time, we had conversations with each other, and when we weren't in the same room, we wrote letters. But that was far too cumbersome, so technology proposed the solution of the telephone call. That worked well for a while, but then technology once again intervened to allow us a more expedient form of communication with the e-mail. But with the rise of carpal tunnel syndrome, the e-mail, too, quickly moved to second place and was replaced by something that was faster and took less effort—an entirely digital conversation through texting, status updates, and tweets.

This book isn't a commentary on the use of technology, but the trend tells us that our human relationships are spreading wider as opposed to deeper. Think about the rich irony of walking into a coffee shop, a place like Starbucks that was founded not only to serve coffee but also to provide an environment outside of the home where people can connect. Walk in, and amidst the scores of lattes and Frappuccinos, with the indie rock playing softly in the background, and what do you see?

Earbuds. Everywhere. And screens popped up.

You see people who are at once all together, and yet all alone. Our interactions with each other have become mindlessly and endlessly ordinary. Perhaps that lack of depth in relationships is why we treat our associations so casually. We trade relationships like baseball cards. When one isn't exciting or fulfilling enough to us, we cash it in and move on, whether that's in marriage, in membership to a church, or even in a run-of-the-mill friendship. Fortunately for us, trading in and out of human association is as easy as changing a relationship status on Facebook.

Our relationships were meant for more. And the "more" is meant to be found not in more exciting relationships, but right in the middle of the everyday ones we already have.

Friendships and Asparagus

Asparagus is a dirty word at our house. It has other dirty word cousins, like green beans and broccoli, but asparagus trumps them all. When our kids see those lovely green stalks roasting in the oven-safe dish, the complaining starts with the first breath. Most of the time, they choke them down, but it's only after a couple of trips to their rooms to "think about it for a while." The cry of loathing goes up with one voice from the table: "I hate asparagus!"

But then there's pizza night. Pizza night is when everyone is excited. It's when a great shout of elation erupts from the mouths of babes, and when second-degree burns hit the rooftops of those same mouths as they begin to shovel it in. The universal cry is similar to what happens on asparagus night in terms of its force:

"I love pizza!"

But *love?* Is that really the right word? In our vocabulary it is, because most of us actually relate to friendships in the same way we broadly relate to food. We love pizza not because of its nutritional value, color, or texture. We love pizza for one reason and one reason only: the taste. We *love* the feeling we get when we take the first bite.

The word we use to describe what pizza means to us is the same word we apply to movies, music, clothes, pets, sports, friendships, and a host of other things. And we use it for essentially the same reason every time: We love how those things make us feel.

As long as that thing, whether it's pizza or a friend, makes us feel good, then the term applies. But as soon as it doesn't, then we revert to the asparagus terminology. The core of most of our relationships, if we're being frank, is about answering the question deeply ingrained within our selfish, greedy hearts: *What can you do for me?*

That question is what blinds us to the extraordinary

within these relationships. It's what makes them drip with the ordinary. It's what has pushed them to be an endless series of surface level texts, all designed to get down to that same issue: *What's in it for me?*

Our relationships were meant for more than this. *We* were meant for more than this. As is the case with so many other everyday, ordinary parts of life, what we need is not to find new relationships. We need to reexamine the extraordinary nature of friendship from the beginning. The answer, I believe, isn't to trade up, but to dig in. So let's start at the beginning.

It Is Not Good for Man to Be Alone

Let me say up front that I am an introvert. That's why, at least part of me, wants to take exception with the statement above: "It is not good for man to be alone." Too bad God was the One who made it. As you roll through the account of creation recorded in Genesis 1 and 2, you see that after everything God made, He reflected that it was good. Yet it's not until He forms man, in His own image, out of the very dust of the earth, and breathed the life of the soul into him that the phrase shifts: "It was *very* good." It was very good, for humanity alone possesses the unique characteristic that the book of Genesis describes as being created in the image of God. Very good indeed.

Yet not finished.

Scholars debate the meaning of the phrase, "image of God" used to uniquely describe the place of humanity in God's creation. Some argue that this image of God is shown through our capacity to create, albeit not in the same fashion as God. Others say the image of God is manifested in the presence of the immortal soul. Still others regard it to mean the higher thinking and cognitive functions of humanity. All are probably true, for all stem from and provide a glimpse into the capacity of God Himself. But there's another component woven into the very fabric of our being too—something that also reflects a key attribute of God.

We are relational creatures.

And we are relational creatures because God is a relational God.

This is not to say that God was lonely or bored in heaven one day (or whatever you might call a "day" before there were days) and thought to Himself that He *needed* a companion. Not so. To think this way calls into question the perfection and self-sufficiency of God.

The Persons of the triune God—Father, Son, and Holy Spirit—exist in perfect and unbroken relational fellowship with each other, within the Trinity, from and for all eternity. God exists in relationship to Himself. To be made in God's image, then, is to be made to relate.

That's why it wasn't good for man to be alone. Being made in the image of God means we were made to mirror the relational capacity of God. And so Adam was given Eve.

Echoes of our relational need are rooted deep inside of us, down past our selfishness and greed in relationships. Why do people congregate together? Why do we know that emotional health is seen not in isolation but in relationships with others? Why is isolation seen as a warning sign of someone on the edge? Because we know, down deep inside of us, that we were meant to be together. This current of togetherness runs throughout the pages of Scripture.

When God called Abram to leave his home and go to a land he had never seen, what was He doing? This was the launching point for the people of God, not the individuals of God. When we were called from darkness into light as Christians, God birthed us into the people of faith. Then there are all of the various commands of the New Testament in which we are called to love one another. Be kind to one another. Give to one another. Gather with one another. It sounds remedial to say, but these commands cannot be lived out in isolation. And when we get to the very end of the story, we don't find humans in heaven worshipping alone but together, accompanied by those from every tribe, tongue, and nation. God wants us to be together.

God has always been building a people for Himself. Though we might have been individually saved, we weren't the only individuals saved. We are part of that people, marked by the blood of Jesus Christ, that will live in fellowship with Him and each other for all eternity. No, it is not good for man to be alone. We were meant for more. It is our eternal destiny to be united with others in the worship of Jesus.

The image should blow our individualistic minds. When we are with others, deeply loving and caring and walking alongside each other, we aren't just hanging out. There is much more at stake. We are mirroring the relationship God has within Himself and we are giving ourselves to the end of all mankind. This is a big deal. It's a much bigger deal than a text message.

How lightly we take the fact that we interact with each other on a daily basis. How we waste our words as if the creatures around us are disposable entities rather than the image bearers of God. In order for us to begin to see the greatness lying within these ordinary, daily interactions, we must embrace the fact that those people around us aren't there to make us feel good; they are not to be used. They are to be treasured and valued. They are to be connected with in a deep and meaningful way as we understand that each one is a representative of God's divine nature on earth.

That's all well and good to say, but what does it look like? Does it mean that every bit of our time is spent in pensive conversation with another? That there's no room for football games? For laughter? For processing through the details of an ordinary day? For small talk? It does not. In C. S. Lewis's words:

> There are no ordinary people. You have never talked to a mere mortal. Nations, cultures, arts, civilizations—these are mortal, and their life is to ours as the life of a gnat. But it is immortals whom we joke with, work with, marry, snub and exploit—immortal horrors or everlasting splendors. This does not mean that we are to be perpetually solemn. We must play. But our merriment must be of that kind (and it is, in fact, the merriest kind) which exists between people who have, from the outset, taken each other seriously—no flippancy, no superiority, no presumption.[2]

There is a certain measure of sobriety we need to approach our fellow men and women with. It's a respect that acknowledges that God has uniquely created this person, each one has a story, and we don't have any idea for what purpose God might have connected us at that given moment.

You Don't Know Who You're Dealing With

The sudden realization that you are not dealing with a mere mortal is a jarring one. It is baffling to think that the same person you order your coffee from is an image bearer of God. It is amazing to consider that the friend you are talking with on the phone will accompany you into the presence of Jesus. And yet you walk around, day by day, as if you are living out some sort of board game, moving the pieces around to suit your own ends, rather than recognizing with sobriety the true greatness of those around you.

You do not know who you are dealing with.

You don't know where they've been. And you certainly don't know where they're going, but that shouldn't matter. This isn't some kind of networking principle, where you should always be nice to those you come in contact with because they might be in a position to advance you someday. The point is that because you are so convinced in God's constant presence and work you can approach all your relationships with faith, believing that you are interacting with someone of great importance in the eyes of God, whether the world around you recognizes that immense value or not.

Armed with this kind of faith, we can take a proactive approach to relationships. We can move from assuming that it's just an ordinary conversation with just another person to the assumption that there is nothing ordinary at all about our daily interactions. This kind of approach is active, rather than passive, and embodies the kind of perspective that Paul advocates in Ephesians 5:15–16: "Pay careful attention, then, to how you walk—not as unwise but as wise—making the most of the time, because the days are evil."

The Bible often uses this word, *walk*, to describe the way we live and move in our daily interactions. We walk through life, one step at a time, and for Paul, that walk should be characterized with a sense of careful- ness. We are to walk carefully. But let's be careful here, lest we misunderstand the kind of carefulness Paul is describing.

Our family lives in a relatively old house, built in the late 1950s. It's a great old home that's been through some renovations in the last years, but through all the gutting and knocking down of walls we've kept the same hardwood flooring that's been there from the beginning. While it's great looking, complete with all the divots and distressing that comes with fifty years of use, it also has some drawbacks. Namely, the noise.

I take great comfort in the fact that as our children grow to be teenagers there won't be any sneaking out of our home because you can't move anywhere without some kind of creak. While that's a great tool for keep- ing potentially ornery teenagers in line, it does make things difficult for the tooth fairy.

When said "fairy" needs to sneak into a kid's room at night and take the tooth from under the pillow, it's often a half-hour task that's marked by stepping on cer- tain carefully planned out places in the floor that don't let out the telltale creak. Those creaks have, more than once, awakened a child who then has wondered why the tooth fairy looks remarkably like dad.

You have to be careful when you walk in our house. Every footfall is made with a painstaking amount of agility for fear that you might just step in the wrong place. That kind of carefulness is defensive in nature. It's like walking on eggshells with sweat beading up on our foreheads to make sure we don't step wrongly. And while it's true that the Christian life demands that we are careful where and how we walk, making sure we are avoiding sin in these evil days, the kind of carefulness that should mark us is much more offensive than defensive in nature. That's the kind of carefulness Paul is advocating in Ephesians 5.

In this careful walking, Paul said that we should make the most of the time we are given. Literally, we are to redeem the time; we are to "buy it back." That's what redemption is. In the case of our common, human interaction, our time has been stolen by our supposed busyness. It's been stolen by our inflated sense of self-importance. It's been inflated by our use and misuse of people for our own ends. This is what needs to be bought back.

When you redeem something, you trade it in for something better. And because of what Jesus has done on the cross, these everyday interactions that come our way as we walk through life can be redeemed. Because we ourselves have been bought back by Jesus at the cross, the way we see everyone else who comes into our path is renewed. Our vision is transformed. We, in a sense, have the ability and the responsibility to look past the surface and on to something deeper. We have, as Christians, the opportunity to see in our fellow humans what they themselves might not even see themselves: "From now on, then, we do not know anyone in a purely human way" (2 Cor. 5:16).

The carefulness with which we walk, then, is not born out of fear that we might be inadvertently involved in some kind of sin, but anticipation. We walk through life with our heads on a swivel, armed by the knowledge of what Jesus has done for us in the gospel and the confidence in the presence and work of God. We are constantly looking this way and that, believing that every interaction is significant. And we are committed to make the most of each one.

When we choose to walk through life with this kind of offensive posture, we are choosing to engage people with the gravity and seriousness that eludes so much of humanity today. We can embrace the God who is constantly transforming the ordinary into the extraordinary through a few carefully but intentionally placed words here or there.

Take the example of Paul. But don't look at him as the man who wrote the bulk of the New Testament. And don't think of him as the theologian who articulated the core doctrines of the Christian faith. Think instead of a man who has just had his entire life turned upside down. Think of him wandering aimlessly, looking for direction. And then think of who God used to propel him forward as an instrument of salvation to the entire known world. Think of the regular guy named Ananias.

Everyone Wants to Be Paul

The story of Paul's conversion is a familiar one. So familiar, in fact, that often we refer to someone's dramatic change of life, after meeting Jesus, even these hundreds of years later, as a "Damascus Road Experience."

Saul, as he was once called, was an ardent opponent of the Christian movement. He was driven by the passionate pursuit of ridding the world of what he thought of as an offense to the Holy God of Israel—the new religious movement of Christians. He traveled, with orders in hand, to imprison and dispatch any of those reckless believers who considered Jesus Christ to be God. But then Saul was literally knocked off his high horse.

In a vision, Jesus Himself appeared to Saul, and suddenly Saul knew the terrible and glorious truth: In his attempts to defend God from blasphemy, he had become a blasphemer himself. But that's just the beginning of the story.

The vision of Jesus had left Saul blinded—an

appropriate metaphor for his life since he had been blinded up to that point to the truth of the gospel. After encountering Jesus on the Damascus Road, Saul was led into the city by his companions who had heard the words of Jesus and yet seen nothing. And there he stayed.

For three days, he was blind. For three days, he neither ate nor drank. For three days, he was left to consider what kind of life he had led, and what kind of life he would lead from that point forward. He spent seventy-two long hours of deep reflection; we can only imagine what must have gone through his mind:

"What have I done?"

"How could I have been so wrong?"

"What do I do now?"

Saul found himself in a place of confusion. A place of darkness. A place of wondering about the nature of the world and his own place in it. As we read the account recorded for us in Acts 9, we picture Saul huddled in a corner of darkness, hungry and thirsty not only for the physical to sustain his body but also for something spiritual to sustain his soul. We might well be wondering where the light would come from.

Luke, the author of Acts, provides the answer for us: "There was a disciple in Damascus named Ananias" (Acts 9:10). That's all we get. We don't have any indication that Ananias had any special education or training. We don't know if he was young or old, what he did for a living, or what his family was like. We have no idea whether he was a man of great or little standing in his community. We only know that he was a follower of Jesus. Just a regular, old disciple that was ready when the Lord called his name:

> And the Lord said to him in a vision,
> "Ananias!" "Here I am, Lord!" he said. "Get up
> and go to the street called Straight," the Lord
> said to him, "to the house of Judas, and ask
> for a man from Tarsus named Saul, since he is
> praying there. In a vision he has seen a man
> named Ananias coming in and placing his
> hands on him so he can regain his sight."
> "Lord," Ananias answered, "I have heard
> from many people about this man, how much
> harm he has done to Your saints in Jerusalem.
> And he has authority here from the chief
> priests to arrest all who call on Your name."
> But the Lord said to him, "Go! For this man
> is My chosen instrument to take My name to
> Gentiles, kings, and the Israelites. I will show
> him how much he must suffer for My name!"
> (Acts 9:10–16)

Ananias was understandably a little nervous about the call. He knew this man's reputation. The city was already buzzing about his imminent arrival and what would happen to the church there. He was apprehensive at best; fearful at worst. But when it came to it, he chose to believe in the power and presence of God, and so he went. And his response, upon meeting Saul, is telling: "Brother Saul, the Lord Jesus, who appeared to you on the road you were traveling, has sent me so that you can regain your sight and be filled with the Holy Spirit" (Acts 9:17).

Brother. How sweet those words must have been to the ears of the blind man. How he must have perked up when he heard them. This was not the voice of self-importance. This was not the sound of arrogance. This, Saul knew, was a friend. This was someone who was indeed sent by Jesus, one who could speak just a little bit of clarity into the ball of confusion that was Saul's life.

And then he was gone.

We have no record of whether Ananias and Saul became pen pals after that moment. We don't know if Ananias went on to do big things in the church and the world. For all we know, this man disappeared from Saul's life as he became Paul the same way he disappears from the pages of Scripture.

Such is the case with our conversations. We are apprehensive. We are fearful. We don't know for sure if we have the right words that can generate impact. We say something, some measure of kindness or encouragement or empathy, and then we disappear from someone's life forever like a vapor in the wind, and there is less than a few lines written about us in books that record history for generations following.

But imagine if there had been no Ananias. Imagine if there had been no moment of clarity. Imagine if that man, huddled in the darkness, had been left there in the darkness. Everyone wants to be Paul. No one wants to be Ananias.

However, we are not all called to be Paul. But all of us are called to be Ananias. As we live and move as relational beings in the midst of these creatures of God, we are meant to push back the darkness and bring light one conversation at a time. We are meant to be looking—and looking with expectation—for where the sovereign hand of God is positioning us. We might not ever gain the notoriety of Paul, but we must move toward the spirit of Ananias. In doing so, we must approach every single interaction, no matter how common and ordinary it might seem, with the same words that characterized this great supporting character in the biopic of the apostle: "Here I am, Lord."

That's what we need. We don't need a bunch of new and exciting relationships, not if we believe in the abiding presence and work of God. We need instead to lay the grid of faith over the top of these ordinary interactions we have day after day. We need to buy the coffee in faith. We need to walk in the grocery store in faith. We need to take the phone call in faith. And if we do, we'll begin to see the extraordinary invading the ordinary.

CHAPTER 6

THE OLD BALL AND CHAIN

The Weight of Marriage

On July 30, 1999, I was twenty years old by about forty-five days. It was the summer before my junior year in college. I had a full load of classes set to begin a month later and a part-time job to go with it. And I found myself standing on the stage of the First Baptist Church in Canyon, Texas, watching Jana Michelle Parker being led down the aisle by her father to be given to me as my bride.

And that's pretty much all I remember.

Once a year we haul out the VHS tape of our wedding and watch as much of it as our three kids will allow before they threaten mutiny, and every single time I watch it, it feels a bit like an out-of-body experience. I vaguely remember putting on a tux. I can sort of recollect moving into position on the steps. But then everything else is a blur, right up until we left the reception.

While the wedding itself is sort of a haze, I remember with absolute clarity the beginning of the honeymoon. No, it's not because of why you think it is. It's instead because I remember the feeling of absolute panic as I woke up in Lake Tahoe, Nevada, a day later.

I'm not overstating that.

Panic. Not the "what have I done" kind of panic, as if I regretted marrying this beautiful woman. Panic brought on by the sheer new weight that I almost immediately began to feel. The honeymoon played out that sense of heightened responsibility.

We both were twenty years old when we tied the knot; that's pretty young by current standards (and getting younger as each day passes). It's old enough to vote, but not old enough to drink, and as it turned out, not old enough to rent a car either. So we found ourselves, for the next seven days, riding trolleys and buses around a city neither of us had been to. I found myself trying to do things I had never done before, like pay a hotel bill and read a city street map to know where we were going. That's what caused the panic.

Up until that point, I had largely been taken care of. My dad always seemed to know the right question to ask, the right person to talk to, the right decision to make, and even the right direction to go on the road. I was a passenger along the way. But now here I was, in an unfamiliar city, with my wife. *My wife!* And suddenly, I was the one who was supposed to know those questions and directions. And I did not.

For the next·year, I was daily confronted by all the things I did not know. I did not know how to pay rent. I did not know what an insurance premium was or how to get one of those. I did not know how to set up the electricity for an apartment or how to plan for retirement (which all the television commercials assured me I needed to be doing). All in all, it was a pretty miserable first year. Starting with the honeymoon, I felt the weight of responsibility shift in my direction. It was, I knew somewhere deep inside, more than just being charge of a household. It was deeper than that. It was heavier than that.

Now, these years later, looking back on that first year, I wonder what I would tell myself if I could speak to me at the front end of that transition. Would I tell myself to relax? To chill out? That all those things aren't a big deal? I actually don't think I would. I think I would tell myself that I should feel that weight.

Marriage is a weighty proposition. To deny the heaviness of it is to deny what makes it wondrous. Perhaps that weightiness is what drives people away from marriage these days.

The Marriage Escape

Marriage, as an institution, is in trouble—that's no secret. Over the last decade, the average age of marriage has gotten progressively later, with more and more people choosing cohabitation or singleness as an alternative to actual and traditional marriage. Then, once inside marriage, more and more people are getting out of it. Divorce rates continue to rise as men and women alike find it easier than ever before to dissolve their union, with no more than "irreconcilable differences" as the excuse.

Let's be honest: marriage can be monotonous. It is, by its very definition, living in the closest proximity imaginable with another human being, and it can be frustrating as you naturally fall into a pattern of behavior. You learn the most intimate traits and aspects of another person, and over time, it can seem that there's nothing left to discover. Marriage can easily get boring. Vanilla. Typical. You know which side of the bed you sleep on and your spouse does too. You settle into a routine of watching the same TV shows, having the same conversations about your day, and even eating the same meals on a regular cycle. You pretty much know what to expect on any given day. To try and deal with that, well-meaning counselors and psychologists often prescribe things like "spicing up" the marriage. Anybody who has been married for more than about three months knows that things like that can be helpful. Something to change the routine. Something to keep things fresh. But if that's the solution, then the assumption is that the underlying problem is one of boredom. If that's so, then the solution might well be as easy as moving hamburger night from Friday to Tuesday or including an extra couple of dates each month.

But what if that's not true? What if the problem isn't boredom? What if we are really trying to escape marriage because of its weight and seriousness? If that is true, then the solution to a typical marriage isn't nearly as simple as "spicing things up." The solution is to reconnect with what we sense inside of us—to understand the gravity of marriage in a deeper way than we have before.

Back to the Beginning

The very first time we see marriage mentioned in Scripture is in Genesis 2. Adam, having been presented with Eve by God, made a profound reflection: "This one, at last, is bone of my bone and flesh of my flesh;

this one will be called 'woman,' for she was taken from man. This is why a man leaves his father and mother and bonds with his wife, and they become one flesh" (Gen. 2:23–24). And marriage was born. These few verses form the foundation of what we still believe to be true about the nature of marriage—that it was instituted by God. That it's the most intimate of relationships imaginable. That the bond formed between man and woman is meant to be unbreakable. There's plenty there to go on, and plenty that contradicts much of the way our society views marriage. But what if that's not the real beginning? What if, in order to grasp the fullness of the gravity of marriage, we actually need to go back further?

But further to what? That's a fair question. We are, after all, dealing with the first two chapters of Scripture here. Before this, there weren't any people to go back to. But there was God. God was further back. And if we keep going, back before God created the antelope and the zebra, back before He breathed life into man or took his rib to make woman, we find the idea of marriage percolating in the heart and mind of God.

Paul helps us go back further in his commentary on Genesis 2. When he was giving instructions to the church at Ephesus about their own marriages, he actually quoted Genesis 2. Then, in commenting on this passage, he remarked: "This mystery is profound, but I am talking about Christ and the church" (Eph. 5:32).

That takes us further back, and further in. Paul, in this one single sentence, opens the door to the great mystery of what's really happening when a man and a woman are joined together in marriage. According to Paul, the great mystery is that marriage isn't at its core about procreation. It's not about companionship. It's not about sex. Marriage is about the gospel.

If you read back through Ephesians 5, you see Paul reflecting on husbands and wives through the gospel lens. Husbands, he says, should treat their wives as Christ treats the church, loving them in a self-sacrificial kind of leadership. Wives, meanwhile, should follow their husbands as the church follows Christ, with confidence in their love and care for them. Simple enough, right? Marriage and the gospel. Husbands and Jesus. Wives and the church. But to really embrace this mystery, we need to consider this question: Does the gospel illustrate marriage, or does marriage illustrate the gospel? The answer is what will really help us grasp the immensity of what we're dealing with here.

Which Came First?

If you have kids, you know the power of an illustration, especially when trying to explain a concept rather than a tangible entity. Let's say that you want to talk to your kids about something like perseverance. That's a concept. So how do you explain something conceptual like that? You look for something tangible as an illustration. We do this in parenting all the time.

One of the things our kids have to do every morning is make their beds. It took a while for them to embrace the act, but now that they've been doing it for a while, it's become a regular part of their routine along with brushing their teeth (most mornings) and combing their hair (most of the other mornings). Here's the thing, though—they aren't very good bedmakers. You don't get a traditional Army tuck and tighten with these kids. You get a bedspread pulled up to the pillows and then awkwardly smoothed out as best they can.

Our daughter has even found a loophole in the bedmaking process. For a couple of years now, she has chosen to sleep on top of her sheets and quilt, only under a small decorative blanket. She will put on hat, gloves, and socks when it gets cold, all because she knows that it's much easier to fold that three-by-three-foot square than all the rest of her covers.

My wife and I don't, on a daily basis, go in and correct their bedmaking. We don't meticulously respread their blankets and straighten their pillows. The highest goal of the exercise isn't to have a neatly made bed; it's to teach them a sense, albeit small, of daily responsibility. The bedmaking is the illustration of the concept. The starting point is the responsibility, and it's the end game as well. First comes the desire to instill responsibility; then comes the illustration meant to emphasize it. The whole exercise is a failure if all they ever learn is how to neatly fold a few sheets.

The order is important.

The question of whether the gospel illustrates marriage, or marriage illustrates the gospel, is important. The answer points us to the highest end of marriage. So the question, in other words, goes like this: Did God institute marriage, and then think to Himself that what He made looks a lot like what He's doing through the relationship between Christ and the church, or did He specifically institute marriage to be illustrative of what He has always had in His mind and heart from the beginning of time in the gospel? The answer is apparent. The gospel is the highest end. Marriage is not. Is it really too much of a stretch to think that God specifically designed marriage, even from the beginning, with this end in mind? Is it too hard to believe that He would have that kind of foresight and intentionality? I don't think it is.

Now we might be tempted to think this truth actually lessens the importance of marriage. It's just an illustration we might argue. It's like making the bed; if it doesn't work, God can find something else to show us to illustrate the relationship between Jesus and the church. But nothing could be further from the truth. The importance of marriage is actually heightened when you see its illustrative relationship to the gospel. We come to understand that marriage cannot be disposable because the gospel is not disposable. Husbands cannot shirk their responsibility because Jesus would never shirk His. Wives cannot get bored and stray because the church is united to Christ. Seeing the gospel as the end serves to propel us into the gravity of what's happening in our typical marriages.

We are doing so much more than eating, drinking, working, parenting, and sleeping together. We have been chosen by the living and eternal God to be the walking, talking, living, breathing representatives of the greatest and most central news in the universe: the gospel of Jesus Christ. That's the weight we all feel deeply inside of us. That's the gravity of marriage. And reconnecting with that truth is how we might begin to see marriage not a series of monotonous actions and choices made day after day but instead as a profoundly significant means God has instituted in order to tangibly represent the great news of the gospel.

Suddenly, it's not just an act of kindness when a husband chooses to do all the dishes; it's a visible example of the way Jesus tangibly serves the people of God. It's not just a few nice words when a wife chooses to verbally encourage her husband's leadership; it's a tangible representation of the confidence that Christians have in following the great leadership of Jesus. It's not just an admirable quality when couples celebrate thirty, forty, or fifty years of marriage; it's a demonstration of the kind of commitment that God has made to all His children, sealing them with the blood of His very own Son. Marriage suddenly gets bigger and weightier than we ever thought possible as even our smallest choices are infused with great meaning.

If the profound mystery of marriage is that it is God's representation of the gospel in visible and tangible terms, then there are at least three key aspects of marriage that we can isolate that serve to highlight the gospel: our differences, our unity, and our commitment.

Differences

Think back to Ephesians 5. As Paul was leading up to the big reveal moment where he articulated the greater purpose of marriage, he highlighted the key differences between the role of the husband and wife inside of a marriage relationship. These aren't popular verses these days, for they're laced with loaded words like "submit" and "rule." We read these verses through a twenty-first-century filter and we think, at first glance, that Paul is advocating a one-sided relationship dominated by the overbearing husband where the dutiful wife spends her days making sandwiches and thinking up ever more elaborate ways to please her man. But read carefully and you see a drastically different picture. It's through embracing the differences in the roles of marriage that the greatness of the gospel becomes apparent.

It's true that Paul calls on the wife to submit to her husband:

> Wives, submit to your own husbands as to the
> Lord, for the husband is the head of the wife
> as Christ is the head of the church. He is the
> Savior of the body. Now as the church submits
> to Christ, so wives are to submit to their hus-
> bands in everything. (Eph. 5:22–24)

But if we have the starting point as the gospel, then the right question to ask first isn't how the wife submits to the husband; it's how the church submits to Jesus. So how does the church submit to Jesus? The church submits willingly and joyfully to Jesus. But let's not stop there. Let's ask the other question that's laying out there: *Why* does the church submit to Jesus?

Now we're getting at the difference in this kind of submission and what we might be tempted to think of submission. The church, when she submits to Jesus, doesn't find herself treated like a doormat. Nor does she find herself robbed of her individual personhood. Far from it. Instead, we find that through submission, the church actually has her individuality lifted up.

Jesus is the One who died and gave individual gifts to the church. He's the One who is devoted to the individual expression of our spiritual gifts and personalities as the Lord has formed and made us. That's why we can confidently, as Christians, submit to the leadership of Jesus Christ. It's because He has proven His great love and care for us, and we know that in submission we aren't actually losing anything; we are instead gaining the fullest expression of who we are.

In marriage, when we see it as the gospel, submission is the pathway to true freedom, not slavery. If a wife is going to joyfully and willingly submit to the loving leadership of her husband, she must be confident that her submission is not going to be abused for her husband's ends. Instead, she should know that she can submit because her husband is going to treat her in the manner that Jesus treats the church.

This kind of submission should cause the husband to tremble. It certainly does me. I know that when we make big decisions in our house, Jana is going to express her opinion. We are going to talk it out, perhaps even too much. But I also know that at the end of all those conversations, she is going to express the same thing to me that she does to Jesus on a daily basis: "I trust you." That does indeed make me tremble. It makes me, above all, want to make sure that I am stewarding that trust as well as I possibly can.

It's with this kind of trembling that husbands ought to read Paul's next command:

Husbands, love your wives, just as Christ loved the church and gave Himself for her to make her holy, cleansing her with the washing of water by the word. He did this to present the church to Himself in splendor, without spot or wrinkle or anything like that, but holy and blameless. In the same way, husbands are to love their wives as their own bodies. He who loves his wife loves himself. For no one ever hates his own flesh but provides and cares for it, just as Christ does for the church, since we are members of His body. (Eph. 5:25–30)

The responsibility of the wife is to submit to the leadership of her husband. It's not because she is of a lesser quality; it's because she is representative of the church. But the husband's job is to emulate Christ in this relationship. He is to love His wife as Jesus loves— to love her sacrificially. To love her unconditionally. To love her beneficially. Husbands, that means that we must be men of initiative in this relationship. We must recognize that leadership is not a choice; it is a given, whether we like it or not. There are all sorts of things like this in life.

You might not have chosen to be an American citizen. You still have to pay taxes.

You might not have chosen to have high cholesterol. You still have to watch how much bacon you eat.

You might not have any interest in being a leader in your home. Sorry about that—you already are one.

In these matters, there's not really a choice. The issue isn't one of opting in or out; it's one of identity. Your home, your church, and your family are led by you. It's part of your DNA. You are leading right now, even if you're not consciously doing so. The question for you and I, husbands, isn't whether or not to lead; it's what direction we want to lead. If we decide we don't want to lead, we won't stop being leaders. We'll just be leading our homes away from faith. Away from the church. Away from respect. Away from responsibility.

We are leaders. It's how we were formed and made, and part of what makes us different. That doesn't mean we have to paint our chests blue and kill animals with sharp sticks. I'm not into either one of those things. Not every man has to lead like that, but every man has to lead somewhere. Like it or not.

It's when we embrace these differences in our roles that we begin to demonstrate the truth of the gospel— that Jesus will not betray the trust we lovingly and willingly place in Him. Indeed, we place that trust in Him because we know He will not betray it.

Unity

It's clear, then, that we have different roles in marriage, and it's through these differences that the gospel is clearly seen. But the gospel is also seen in the way we are bonded together in unity. Did you notice how the book of Genesis, and later Paul, were careful to help us see how closely men and women are united in marriage? They become *one flesh*. And while that phrase has a sexual connotation to it, it's more about intimacy and unity than a sexual relationship.

We are absolutely unified in marriage. We are inseparable, until death do us part. In the same way that we wouldn't cut off part of our own flesh, we cannot remove our partner in marriage. We are together.

There's a simple phrase that Jana and I repeat to each other, almost like a mantra, that helps us to remember this: *We are on the same team.* Let me paint a picture for you from our house to show what that means.

It's late in the day, the witching hour for parents with young children. The kids are rebelling against the "green stuff" on their plates, claiming that if they simply must eat something of that color, then Skittles has a lovely variation that fits the bill.

It's been a long day at work, full of copy machine jams, meetings that went thirty minutes too long, e-mails, and overdemanding bosses. It's been an equally long day at home with school pickups, homework assignments, potty training, piano lessons, and preparation of the aforementioned "green stuff."

In short, everyone is ready to snap, including Mom

and Dad. It seems inevitable that someone is leaving that table in tears, their emotional nose bloodied by a well-placed verbal jab. This phrase above is particularly powerful to get through such times, when the nerves of both my wife and I are frayed to the breaking point: "We're on the same team."

That's easy to forget during the witching hour, when baths have to be taken, dishes have to be done, and everyone is a little overextended from the day. It's during the witching hour that, in my selfishness, I can easily convince myself that I stand alone. That the children have conspired against me to make my life harder. That my spouse doesn't understand the burdens and pressures of my life. That I am a lone ranger in the house.

But I'm not. And my wife reminds me I'm not.

"We're on the same team."

Suddenly I realize my foolishness. There is no nefarious motive behind the question to help with the dishes. There is no evil intent behind the request to bathe the kids.

"We're on the same team."

God has joined us together in this fight—the fight for our home, for order, for the extension of grace. And what God has joined together, no man should separate. Least of all me. But that's exactly what I'm trying to do when I firmly assume my status as the nightly martyr. It's our unity, during the simple times like these, that shows forth the gospel in our marriages. And if we are on the same team at dinner time, we are going to be on the same team through job changes, disease, loss, financial decisions, and a host of other shifts in life's equilibrium.

Remember, husbands. Remember, wives: You're on the same team. You're not being internally and subversively sabotaged. Remember it, and tell it to each other. Feel the weight begin to lift. Look back at the paranoia with which you have been afflicted. Believe in the good intentions of your spouse. Embrace that God has given you the gift of each other, and come at life with a unified front.

Commitment

Commitment is what brings the embracing of our differences and our unity together. Commitment is what abides when the sheen is worn off love. Indeed, commitment is what makes love truly love. It is commitment that endures—not affection.

Gustave Flaubert, the French writer most famous for his first published work *Madame Bovary*, once said, "One can be the master of what one does, but never of what one feels." In other words, you can exercise some control by sheer will over your actions, but feelings? Well that's a different story. You can't control what you feel. You feel what you feel, and because you feel what you feel, it's like spitting into the wind to try and control it. That's the predominant philosophy most of us tend to take toward marriage. You fall in love with someone, but over time, you fall out of love. Feelings fade. So you just have to move on because you can't generate your feelings.

Right?

Yes, I think. At least in part. But like so many other things, we can be paralyzed into inaction by stopping with these uncontrollable feelings. What happens when you feel one way, and yet you know you should feel something else? What happens when you know, for example, that you should not be angry with your husband or your wife, or with your kids, and yet you feel angry anyway? You know there is no basis for your hostility, and yet there you are, fuming with rage.

What do you do then? Do you simply let yourself fizzle out? Do you wait to do something until you feel something different? If you operate under the above philosophy then the answer is yes. You put yourself at the mercy of your feelings because, after all, what can you really do about those? . . .

You can't do anything except act anyway. You can choose to speak truth to your feelings rather than let them speak truth to you. You can take action, even when (and maybe most especially because) your feelings contradict what you know to be true.

You apologize. Or you forgive. Or you sacrifice. You do so not because you feel like it; you do so because it is good and right and true. Your commitment takes over and you act not out of affection but instead out of faith.

You don't feel like apologizing, forgiving, or sacrificing. Or obeying, for that matter. In short, then, you acknowledge what you feel to be real, and yet you submit yourself to a greater reality. A higher calling. A more important truth. You refuse to be governed by what your senses tell you, in the moment, and instead believe something different. That belief is strong enough to look contrary feelings in the eye and not blink. At all.

And you know what? A funny thing usually happens. You start to feel differently. Notice, though, that you don't feel differently before you act, but as a result of acting. In this way, it seems, you bring the weight of the authority of Jesus Christ slamming down on your momentary emotions. And what you find, time and time again, especially as your heart begins to change, is that in this domain—the domain of the emotions—Jesus is still Lord.

Commitment trumps affection in marriage. It must be so if we are to mirror the gospel in those marriages. When we act anyway, contrary to our feelings, we are acknowledging that what we know is bigger than what we feel. And what we know is that Jesus is Lord.

There is no such thing as a typical marriage because the gospel is anything but typical. When we catch vision and sight of that extraordinary work of Jesus and begin to approach marriage with it squarely fixed in our mind, it doesn't mean that we won't eat the same things day after day. It doesn't mean that the routine will dramatically change. It certainly doesn't mean that the quirks of our spouses will suddenly go away. It means that we can begin to see the extraordinary nature of this typical marriage that has been waiting there all along.

CHAPTER 7

KIDS WILL BE KIDS

I have not slept past 6:48 a.m. in eight and a half years. It hasn't always been like that; I remember Saturdays in my teens when I would regularly snooze until 10 a.m. or later, waking up just in time for McDonald's to roll their breakfast menu over to lunch. But eight and a half years ago it all changed because that's when we had our first child.

Ever since our oldest son was able to read a clock, we have put a 7 a.m. reverse curfew on our children, telling them with all the seriousness and gravity we can muster that they are not allowed to get out of their rooms until that magic time of day which marks the beginning. What we've learned along the way is that our children don't really care how late a night we've had. They don't care if we've been up most of the night cleaning up the vomit of one of their siblings. They don't care if it's been a particularly hard week and that it's Saturday. They don't even care that *they* went to bed late. They are going to get up at 7 a.m., and 7 a.m. is the beginning of what doesn't shut down until at least 8 p.m. that night.

All the time in between is spent in various forms of household management. Cereal is consumed, diapers are changed, lunches are made, and hair is combed before school. Homework has to be done, and countless miles are driven between dance, Cub Scouts, play dates, birthday parties, and soccer practices. Dinner has to be prepared, the piano must be practiced, and the baths have to be taken. On and on it goes, starting over every single morning at 7 a.m.

I'm relying on secondhand knowledge at this point, but I have heard that the busyness and routine of the schedule does not get better but worse, only shifting to different levels of activities as the children grow. Eventually, then, there are the keys to be handed over, the curfews to be enforced, the colleges to be applied for, and the late nights to wait up during. Such is the life of the parent.

Parenthood is a massive series of monotonous and repeated acts. Over and over again. Day in and day out.

Sometimes I look at my wife and wonder, in light of the 90 percent of her time she spends doing these cyclical things, how in the world she's still sane.

But that is the nature of parenting. You say the same thing, and then you say it over again. The same discipline is passed out for the same transgressions. The same reminders are given about the same items. The same warnings are issued about everything from wiping your nose to not putting the fork in the light socket. If ever there was one area of life that is the epitome of routine and boredom, surely it's this. However, when we read about parenting in the Bible, some very interesting and unexpected language is used to describe it. Not boredom and ordinariness language, but the language of warfare.

Arrows

I've only shot a bow and arrow one time. We were in my brother-in-law's backyard, and he had a target set up about twenty yards away. He had purchased the bow and arrow to hunt with, and he and I along with several kids in tow went together into the yard for a demonstration.

I should be clear at this point—I'm not a hunter. I tried to hunt pheasant one time, but after about forty-five minutes I got cold and bored and wound up sitting in a truck for the rest of the morning. Since then, the closest I've come to firing a weapon was the twin Nerf Blasters I bought for my son and I so we could pelt each other mercilessly with foam darts. Nevertheless, I had seen *Robin Hood* and was curious to see if there was a master marksman somewhere inside me.

There is not.

Even at just twenty feet, my arrow went not left, and not right, but short, to the snickers of my son and nephew. Thus was the unceremonious end of my career as a bow hunter. That's also maybe why the metaphor the psalmist employs in Psalm 127:3–5 is a little difficult for me to understand:

> Sons are indeed a heritage from the LORD,
> children, a reward. Like arrows in the hand
> of a warrior are the sons born in one's youth.
> Happy is the man who has filled his quiver
> with them. Such men will never be put to
> shame when they speak with their enemies at
> the city gate.

At first that passage seems pretty straightforward, acknowledging the great truth that children really are an amazing blessing, a heritage, and a reward from the Lord. But just when you expect the psalm to turn a little sloppy with hugs and kisses all around, we come to some different imagery. Battle imagery. Pictures of war and engagement.

The children aren't only pictured as a reward; they

are seen by the psalmist as a weapon. And in that single picture, we as parents are rocked from the seeming boredom and drudgery of an endless line of dirty diapers. Our children are pictured as weapons. If we want something bigger, something more exciting, something that changes the course of history, then those diapers really matter. If our children are arrows, then we must realize as common, everyday mommies and daddies that our best opportunity to significantly impact the world might just be through our children.

If we can raise them to be kingdom people, people who follow and love Jesus more than they love their lives, then the world can be changed. They can change it, and I can change it vicariously through them. They can become more—more than me, more than businessmen and women, more than pursuers of the American dream—they can become arrows. This is the great task that God has entrusted to us, the wipers of the noses and the fashioners of the ponytails. The washers of the underwear and checkers of the math homework. We as parents have the greatest measure of influence as to how straight they are shot, and how sharp their blades are. We can raise them to understand the great purposes of the universe, and that a life given for those purposes is not one spent in vain.

But the word that stands out to me in the text isn't so much the word *arrow*, though it's inspiring to see my children like that. The word that stands out to me the most is *warrior.* Children are arrows, shot straight into the heart of darkness for the great purposes of God, but they are done so not on their own. Arrows are only pointy sticks if left in the quiver. But put those arrows in the hands of a warrior? Well, then you've really got something.

Warrior is a word of skill. Of courage. Of purpose. The arrows are only arrows; the impacting factor is really about whose hands those arrows are in. The question for us as ordinary parents, doing the ordinary stuff of life, is whether we will be parental warriors or mere managers of time and activities.

As with so many other areas of life, the significance of parenting isn't found outside of the normal everyday stuff; it's actually found inside it. In the laundry. In the peanut butter and jelly. Right in the middle of the routine. The difference between a warrior and a schedule manager is more about perspective than it is about activity. It's about choosing to live, with your children, with a great sense of intentionality and purpose rather than simply trying to get through the day. So for the rest of this chapter, I'd like to humbly suggest four keys for us as parents to aid our perspective in order that we might raise our kids intentionally, right in the middle of the everyday.

Embrace Your Role

We, as parents, are the primary influence in the lives of these children God has given to us. We shape their definitions of justice, fairness, good, evil, and grace. The most sobering part about that formation is that it is happening whether we recognize it or not. We are always teaching regardless of how cognizant we are of that fact.

Coming to that understanding can be more than a little bit jarring, but it happens in the very first hours you become a parent. I remember when Joshua, our first son, was born. After his delivery, these wonderful nurses came to the room, cleaned him up, weighed him, and then took him away. My wife and I ate steak for dinner, watched a little television, and then went to sleep, only to be awakened a couple of times during the night when those same sweet nurses brought our son back to the room so we (and by we I mean she) could feed him.

That was day 1. And then came day 2.

Everything was great in the morning; a steady stream of friends and family came by, all impressed by our handsome little boy who seemed so well behaved. We ate a great breakfast and had a leisurely morning. Then, just after lunch, came checkout time.

One of the nurses wheeled my wife out of the front door of the hospital in a wheelchair. I followed proudly behind with our suitcases, balloons, and gifts. We got to the corner, Jana got up from the wheelchair, and the nurse said good-bye and walked back inside.

All of a sudden, we were alone. Just like that. I went to get the car, and then immediately had a panic attack as I opened the car door, for there it was, staring me in the face. The car seat.

What were the snaps? What were these buckles? Was it supposed to fit like this? Why did his head keep flopping sideways? It was an awkward day in Birmingham traffic as the red SUV with its flashers on made its way down the interstate at twenty-five miles per hour. We were parents. Forever. Everything completely different than it was. We were solely responsible for this other human life, like it or not.

Now that fact can either be absolutely paralyzing or incredibly motivating. By God's grace, it will be the latter, and we will rise to the occasion. But rising to the occasion doesn't mean perfection; it means awareness. The mistakes will come; God knows they will come tomorrow or sooner. But even those mistakes provide an opportunity to model what true sorrow, contrition, and humble repentance look like. We must fully embrace our role as parents, and while that means an incredible amount of joy, it also means something else: death. And if I may say it, it means death especially for fathers.

Dads, you are dead men walking.

According to Jesus, something has to die in order

for something else to live: "I tell you the truth, unless a kernel of wheat falls to the ground and dies, it remains only a single seed. But if it dies, it produces many seeds" (John 12:24 NIV). Of course, we know this verse in its context is most importantly seen in the death of Jesus: Jesus died so that all who believe in Him might live. But it occurs to me that this principle is applicable particularly to fathers whom God has entrusted with the leadership of a family.

We, dads, as the leaders, are the ones who choose to die daily to ourselves so that our family might live. That death works itself out in all kinds of practical ways. It means you wake up earlier than anyone else in the house so that you can have the family devotion ready at the breakfast table. You die to your desire for sleep so that the kids might have life through the Word of God.

It means you choose to learn all you can about basketball even though you don't enjoy playing so that you can help coach your son or daughter's team. You die to your desire for your children to be interested in the same things you are so they might have life in their own God-given talents.

It means you choose to get up day after day and go to work even though you think you might want to quit your job. You die to your desire to see your own dreams fulfilled in order that your family might live and thrive in security.

Fathers, we are dead men walking. We, as the leaders of our homes, are also the ones who are the most willing to step to the front of the line to take the hit. Dying is more than just being willing to give up our lives for the sake of those we love. It's fleshed out in a thousand little choices day after day whereby we take the sacrifice joyfully into ourselves for the sake of another. Death, in this sense, isn't just one big choice. It's something continually done. And because it is, the only real way we are able to take the tiny pinpricks of death over and over again is by remembering that Jesus has done so for us. He died. We live. And now He has entrusted the work of dying to us for the sake of our families. If we want to be warriors, then we must be willing to die. That's what it means to soberly embrace the role God has given to us.

A Heightened Sense of Awareness

To find the great significance in the everyday aspects of life as a parent, we must embrace the great role of responsibility given to us by God. In so doing, we must also begin to live with a heightened sense of awareness. We must realize that there are indeed no wasted moments with our children, though wasteful might seem like the only thing that many of these moments are.

Take something as simple as a home improvement project. Now, to be honest, I'm not a master craftsman.

Come to think of it, I'm not really a minor craftsman.

Our house and yard are full of things that are "good 'nough." The retaining wall isn't quite straight. The baseboard painting project *almost* got all the nail holes covered. The entertainment center has one upside-down door. The swing set didn't really get waterproofed and stained. All passable; none professional.

But for most of these projects, the imperfections are a mark of shame on my part because they're not great. I look at them and see all the imperfections that could have been remedied if I were a better craftsman. They could have been, however, a mark of honor, something that brings a smile every time I see them rather than a shake of the head and a mental, *I should have . . .*

It all depends on whether we are willing to take the time and effort to intentionally engage with our kids over these mundane things. Our three children are endlessly curious. They still, thank God, want to be with and hang around their parents. And they would love to have a paintbrush or a hammer or a set of instructions written in another language in their hands. But I don't let them do that enough.

No, because of my impatience, I'm more likely to wait until they're in bed or plop them in front of a cartoon while I work on the project. But there's a better way, I think. The better way is to invite them in. To equip them with the cool tools they will need. But that's difficult for someone like me, because it's going to take longer. I'll have to explain things over and over again, and they won't be able to work as fast as an adult could. What's more, it's probably going to get messed up at some point, and I'll have to patiently explain (if I know) what we did wrong, and then go back and do it again. It's going to be messy too, because paint and errant hammers will inevitably start flying.

But the benefit? Well . . .

The benefit won't be the perfect bookshelf. It will instead be one with nicks and cracks and nail holes where they shouldn't be. But something tells me that if I actually take the time to put together that thing, whatever it is, I won't have a problem putting it in my yard, or in the living room, or on the table, even though it's not perfect. In fact, my sneaking suspicion is that it will probably stay rooted to its place far longer than some of my other hastily completed projects. We could look at that leaning shelf in the corner, the one that can only really hold the paperbacks, and be able to say together, "Remember when . . ."

These are opportunities for time, influence, and teaching to be seized, not outside the ordinary, but right in the middle of it. But to seize them we must see them. And to see them we must be actively on the lookout for them. That sounds a lot more solidly built than my leaning retaining wall.

Intentional Time

In addition to being aware of the opportunities with our children that are right in front of us, we must also bring a great sense of intentionality to bear in creating specific times with our children. I have dreams about what this might look like for our family: A yearly fancy daddy-daughter Christmas date. An annual camping trip with just me and the boys. Traditions we build around holidays and other special occasions. But let's start even smaller than that. Maybe the most basic intentional time we can create with our kids is establishing a regular time of family devotion.

About a year prior to writing this book, our family began to have a regular time of Bible reading and prayer. We decided it would work best for us, at this stage of life, to do so first thing in the morning during breakfast. And so every day, we would haul out the Bible and our devotion guide, and over waffles or instant oatmeal or Cheerios we would walk through a Bible story together and process it together with the kids.

It has not always gone well.

There was the day we started talking about Noah's ark and then devolved into a discussion about the massive amount of elephant poop there would have been to deal with. Then there was the very intellectually stimulating discussion surrounding how bad-smelling a preacher Jonah must have been after having been vomited up by a giant fish. Oh, and I can't forget the day that we were walking through the story of Jesus and the woman of, um, shall we say questionable reputation, and trying to explain what she was doing that was so bad that people wanted to throw rocks at her until she died.

That was fun.

But then there was the day when we came to the story recorded in Joshua 2 where the Israelites were on the verge of invading the land promised to them by God. They sent spies into the promised land on a clandestine information-gathering mission. The spies were found out, and in order to elude capture, sought refuge with a woman named Rahab. As an expression of their gratitude, the spies told her that she would be saved from the coming destruction of the city. But how was she saved? This is where the conversation at breakfast got really interesting. She was saved because she put a red cord on her window, marking her house to be spared. Almost on a whim, we asked our young children a few deeper questions about that cord, and we were knocked on our spiritual backsides by their response.

"Guys, why was Rahab saved?"

"Because she put the red cord out her window."

"Do you guys remember any other people who put something red on their doors?" And without looking up from his cereal, like it was no big deal, our seven-year-old spouted off:

"Yeah. Like when that angel killed people." He was talking about the Passover. It was a story we had read over that same table eating that same cereal months before. So we probed a little more:

"It was the Passover. And why was that called the Passover?"

"Because the angel passed over their houses."

"And what did the Israelite army do to Rahab's house?"

"They passed over it."

Then came the kicker. "Guys, you know we are still saved today by something red." Everyone was slurping down the last of the cereal-flavored milk at this point. We pressed it a little more: "What is the something red that saves us?"

"Jesus' blood." And suddenly, there, over breakfast, children were articulating the truth of the gospel, but also how that truth runs throughout the whole of the Bible. They were seeing the link between the Old and New Testaments. The crazy part was that the truth of God's Word had found its way past the elephant poop and the fish vomit and landed straight into the minds and the hearts of these children.

There are spiritual moments with your children that are paper thin, and they don't seem to happen that often. It's those times when you really sense they are understanding the nature of sin and our great need for forgiveness, and then they're thinking about Pokémon again. These moments are extraordinarily thin, but they are there to be seized upon if we are ready. The thing is, though, those moments don't just pop out of nowhere. They are, in a sense, manufactured through a commitment to the daily routine. They are hard fought and won through getting up early to make sure breakfast is on the table so you're not rushing around. They are created through showing up around that table day in and day out. They are born from the tedious acts of doing the same thing, day after day after day.

A Commitment to the Gospel

It sounds simple to the point of redundancy, but the greatest thing we might ever do as parents is to hold an unswerving commitment to the gospel above all things. But this commitment to the gospel is not only what our children need to see and hear from us the most; it is what will personally empower us to continue to push on in the most boring and difficult days of parenting.

That means more than telling our children the story of Jesus, though it certainly does mean that. It means being students of our children so that we might know how to best explain the gospel to them. Take, for example, the conversation that occurred at our house at dinner the other night. Our son, when he was confronted (again) with the answer of "no" for something he wanted to do (I think it involved eating peas), responded like this:

"I wish there were no rules."

He's living under the mind-set right now that the rules are there to cramp his style. They deny him freedom to do what he really wants to do and if all these restraints were lifted, his life would be much happier.

This is a lie ingrained into our hearts.

"I love the rules."

That's what his sister, sitting across from him, said with a glint of pride in her eye. She lives to please authority right now, and does not think of herself as sinful in any way, shape, or form. Obeying fills her with pride, and she can't imagine that anything in her heart might need to be changed because she is very proficient at following the rules. If, in fact, there were more and more rules she would be much happier because she would know exactly what the minimum was expected of her and she could perform accordingly.

This, too, is a lie ingrained into our hearts.

Licentiousness and legalism sitting there together at the kitchen table, one believing that the rules deny him happiness and one believing that the rules justify her.

And the gospel is for both. Thank God the gospel frees us from the lie that sin is freedom and happiness and moves us toward the joy of obedience and intimacy. And thank God the gospel frees us from the lie that we are "okay" and makes us into the humble people that are "okay" because of Christ alone. They both need Jesus, but the way they see that need is going to be, I predict, very different from each other.

We, as parents, must recognize these differences, but those differences require no less need. And we must help our children see this. We do that through what we teach, but also how we act. We do it by picking our battles carefully so we do not provoke our children to anger. We do it by making sure that we are truly disciplining our children and not punishing out of frustration. We do it by expressing, over and over again, our immense pride in who they are. And when we fail to do any and all of these things, we do it not by justifying our actions, but by humbly asking their forgiveness.

In those moments, we remember that the good news of Jesus is not just for these children. It's for moms and dads who, from one day to another, need grace to love their children in good and hard ways through all of the ordinary stuff of life.

Imagine . . .

With our kids, as with the rest of our lives, the extraordinary is there. Not outside of the normal, but within us. It's at the kitchen table and at the bedside. It's in the home project and the Bible stories. It's in the changing of diapers and the making of lunches. It's in these common, everyday actions through which we might become warriors and our children might become arrows.

Imagine what they might be in the hands of an extraordinary God. Dream about it. For example, think with me for a minute about that one thing in your child that can both lift your heart and make you roll your eyes. One thing that makes your child unique—intense focus, stubbornness, creativity, the complexity of their minds. That one unique thing.

Right now, that unique characteristic might be frustrating. You may get mad when you have to fight to take the focus off the television, or when you try countless times to logically explain a situation only to realize they are still committed to their own ideas. It might be endlessly aggravating that they always seem to be putting off the small chores like making the bed or cleaning the toothpaste out of the sink.

Instead of thinking about what that character trait looks like right now, think of what that same characteristic might look like having been filtered through the redemptive hands of God in Jesus Christ.

Think of the perseverance that redeemed stubbornness might come to, as your hard-headed son or daughter stays in a marriage or in a church twenty years from now even as it becomes difficult.

Think of the focus that redeemed single-mindedness might come to, as your TV-watching child ruthlessly keeps their eyes fixed on Jesus no matter what it costs them. Think of the courage that redeemed recklessness might come to, as your accident-prone little boy or girl shamelessly speaks words of hope to those around them in their future life.

Think of that, and then feel your heart and soul begin to lift. That's what redemption looks like. It's God, taking these characteristics that, apart from Him, are expressed in greed, laziness, and self-centeredness, but then transforming them into something more. It's not that the characteristic itself changes; it's that God gives them an appropriate avenue for the expression of that characteristic.

Think of Paul, who described himself like this beginning in Philippians 3:12 (NIV):

Not that I have already obtained all this, or have already been made perfect, but I press on to take hold of that for which Christ Jesus took hold of me. Brothers, I do not consider myself yet to have taken hold of it. But one thing I do: forgetting what is behind and straining toward what is ahead, I press on toward the goal to

win the prize for which God has called me
heavenward in Christ Jesus.

The crazy part is how active and vigorous the verb
is that Paul uses in verses 12 and 14. He says that he
is pressing on. In verse 14 it has a competitive, athletic contest feel to it. Maybe Paul was thinking of the
Olympic Games which would have been a familiar sight
to the Greek Philippians. Those games were originally
made up of footraces, and in those races the athletes
would have to strain at the end, pressing hard toward
the goal. The verbs mean to pursue. They mean to run
hard. They mean to focus your energy and your effort.
In fact, they are so vigorous, so competitive, even so
violent, that they can be translated as *persecute*. It is the
same verb, in fact, that Paul uses a participle of in verse
6 to describe himself before meeting Jesus. Then, he
was "persecuting" the church.

For Paul, zeal—even to the point of obsession—was
neutral. The question is not about zeal; it is about the
object of that zeal and whether it is deserving of obsession. For the difference between Paul's life then and
Paul's life after becoming a Christian was not his level
of addiction. If anything, he was more preoccupied
post-Christ than he was before. The difference is that
he finally found something worth his obsession. His
passion remained, but it was redeemed.

May it be with our children. May it be that those
things which cause us daily frustration might move us

to prayer as we dream about what those traits might become in the hands of a redemptive God.

These little boys and girls are arrows in waiting. Will we be the warriors who can fire them? Warriors are made in the ordinary, refined by the mundane. They are crafted through the unremarkable, but their aim is straight and true.

CHAPTER 8

THE ALMIGHTY DOLLAR

$28,000

In the summer of 2000, my young wife and I moved from the small town of Canyon, Texas, and the area of the country where our whole family had always lived to the city of Birmingham, Alabama, so that I could attend Beeson Divinity School. We pulled into our apartment complex with one single truck and an acceptance letter to graduate school. No jobs. No big plan. Just a little youthful confidence that everything would work itself out when we got there.

The day after we moved in, I spent the morning trying to put together an entertainment center we had purchased from the Target down the road while my wife went to an interview for a sixth grade teaching position she had applied for in a local school district. When she walked in the door of our new apartment a few hours later, we left the pieces of the aforementioned entertainment center sitting on the ground to celebrate, because we now had two pieces of paper. In addition to my acceptance letter to graduate school, we had a signed teaching contract for Jana.

They were going to pay her $28,000 a year to further the young minds of Homewood, Alabama. And there was a great cry of joy that went up from the apartment that day.

$28,000 a year! We couldn't believe it. It seemed like an enormous amount of money to us. We went to Pizza Hut that night and *both* of us got the buffet. Times were good, and they continued to be good. Even though the money seemed huge, we knew that we had to live pretty strictly to stay inside that amount. So we would, each day, determine which one of us had to drive the furthest and make sure that person took the 4-cylinder Nissan instead of the 6-cylinder GMC. We spent a lot of evenings eating Totino's pizza and boxed mac and cheese that didn't do very much for our waistlines, but did allow us to have a dinner that cost approximately $1.95. We gave each other an allowance—money that we could spend at our own discretion on anything from a coke to eating a meal out for lunch. It was $20 per month. I would meticulously record each expenditure in our check record, concerned that we were tracking every dime and penny to make the most of what we had. I was, in short, very concerned about money in those days.

I still am very concerned about money these years later, sometimes to the chagrin of my family. I wouldn't say I'm cheap (though I'm pretty sure others would), but I did once bring my wife a Ficus tree that I found near a dumpster. I still am reluctant to turn on the heat in our house until after November 1 and can't stand cranking the air conditioner until May. I still am the guy who goes immediately to the sale rack at TJ Maxx because the secondhand full price seems too expensive. I still track the expenditures of our family and keep a near daily watch on the account balance. What I'm finding is that it's a lot to keep up with because money is the stuff of everyday, ordinary life. You can go virtually nowhere and do virtually nothing without money being in the picture at some point. As boring as all the mundane details of life are, they all have to be funded. The toilet paper has to be bought. The snacks for the kids have to be purchased. The electric bill has to be paid. All these things happen every single day, and they all involve money at some point or another.

Admittedly, all these financial details can get more than a little tedious and boring. They can all begin to fade into a sea of electronic bank transactions, insurance premiums, and mortgage payments. But inside of all of this financial haze is a tremendous amount of significance and importance. The extraordinary is waiting here too, if we take the time and energy to become cognizant of it.

God Cares about Money

The great significance of money is revealed, if by nothing else, by the frequency with which Jesus addressed it. Jesus talked about money more than He did heaven and hell combined. The only other subject He addressed more often than money was the kingdom of God. Eleven of His thirty-nine recorded parables address money in some way, and in the Gospel of Luke, one of every seven verses is about the subject. Jesus cared about money. A lot. Apparently, money is not just a matter of a few bucks here and there. It's not just about paying the bills and buying the groceries. There is something profoundly important going on here right in the middle of the debit cards. If we want to find the significance lurking inside this very ordinary and everyday part of life, we need to dig into the mind and the heart of God and probe just why it is that money matters so much to Him.

Some might say God needs our money. But even as we read that sentence, we see two words that do not belong anywhere in the same vicinity as each other:

"God" and "need." God, by His very nature, is the Giver of all things. He is the Creator and Sustainer of all creation. He is completely self-sufficient in any and every way; He does not need our accolades or our companionship, much less a few pieces of paper or some spare change. God is not some kind of sweating televangelist, constantly begging for funds to get new upholstery on His private jet. One of the most powerful passages that points us to this truth is Psalm 50, a song that reminds us of the great sufficiency of God:

> "Listen, My people, and I will speak; I will
> testify against you, Israel. I am God, your
> God. I do not rebuke you for your sacrifices
> or your burnt offerings, which are continually
> before Me. I will not accept a bull from your
> household or male goats from your pens, for
> every animal of the forest is Mine, the cattle
> on a thousand hills. I know every bird of the
> mountains, and the creatures of the field are
> Mine. If I were hungry, I would not tell you,
> for the world and everything in it is Mine."
> (Ps. 50:7–12)

The people in the Old Testament were treating their sacrifices as spiritual currency. They were operating under the delusion that there is some kind of cosmic flea market where God was willing to barter His blessings for some slaughtered animals. And God comes back with the great truth that is so easy for us to forget in our relative prosperity: "You are not giving Me anything that's not already Mine."

Paul echoed the sentiment in his culminating statement of the first eleven chapters of Romans: "Oh the depths of the riches both of the wisdom and the knowledge of God! How unsearchable His judgments and untraceable His ways! For who has known the mind of the Lord? Or who has been His counselor? Or who has ever first given to Him, and has to be repaid? For from Him and through Him and to Him are all things. To Him be the glory forever. Amen" (Rom. 11:33–36). Amen indeed.

The truth is that no money or anything else we have is really ours; we are caretakers of what God has entrusted to it: "The God who made the world and everything in it—He is Lord of heaven and earth and does not live in shrines made by hands. Neither is He served by human hands, as though He needed anything, since He Himself gives everyone life and breath and all things" (Acts 17:24–25). Ultimately, we are merely stewards of what God has entrusted to us. We are walking through life on borrowed time, borrowed legs, using borrowed money.

God cares deeply about money not because He needs it. He cares about it because of what money reveals about us. Jesus knows this even better than we do. In His various teachings about money, Jesus says things like, "Don't collect for yourselves treasures on earth, where moth and rust destroy and where thieves break in and steal" (Matt. 6:19). He says to the one who wanted to follow Him, claiming He had fulfilled the demands of the law: "You lack one thing: Go, sell all you have and give it to the poor, and you will have treasure in heaven. Then come, follow Me" (Mark 10:21). Did He make these statements because Jesus wanted His followers to be poor? Not necessarily.

Look through the Scriptures and you find many examples of people of great power and resources being held up as examples of faith and following. Abraham was incredibly wealthy. Job was too, and then after his ordeal, his wealth was restored. Cornelius was likely a man of some means who came to be a Christian. Jesus' own ministry was supported by people who did not sell everything they had but instead provided the financial means for He and His disciples to travel and preach. It's not that Jesus wants His followers to be poor; it's that Jesus knows that our bank account is a window to our hearts. Our view of money is perhaps the clearest gauge of what we hold most dear.

Jesus isn't the only One who knows this. Every good marketer knows it too. Think about the constant barrage of advertising messages for products and services. Think of the innumerable radio spots, TV

commercials, billboards, and even Facebook advertise-
ments. Are the good ones—the most effective ones—
about the product they are selling, or are they instead
about something else entirely?

The answer, of course, is the latter. There is an
appeal not only to the taste of the cheese-smothered
chicken or the clarity of the high-definition picture;
there is an attempt to convince you through both
images and explicit messaging that your life is somehow incomplete unless you eat this steak or drink this
beer. That you are somehow missing out if you don't
have this suit or see this movie. Now none of us are
dumb enough to actually say that our lives are incomplete because we don't have an iPhone, but still there
is something that resonates to that effect deep in our
hearts. These are emotional appeals not logical ones,
and most of us end up acting in line with our hearts
rather than our minds.

This is what money reveals—not what we know but
what we believe. Not what's in our minds but what's
in our hearts. That's why Jesus is so concerned about
money. It's not out of greed or need; it's because He
knows that despite what we might say, the true barom-
eter of hearts is measured in dollars and cents.

In our hearts, we find two key aspects with which
God is vitally concerned. They are two things that walk
hand in hand, and two key things that God is winning
back through the gospel: our love and our faith. The

way we spend our money reveals what we love and it reveals what we truly believe.

Our Love

The way we spend our money reveals what we love. In Jesus' mind, money is the primary competitor to the love we have for God: "No one can be a slave of two masters, since either he will hate one and love the other, or be devoted to one and despise the other. You cannot be slaves of God and of money" (Matt. 6:24). There's not a lot of wiggle room in this verse. To Jesus, it's an either/or dynamic.

Every person on earth is going to be mastered by something. The question is not so much whether we will be enslaved but what we will be enslaved by. Jesus characterizes the life of the disciple as one of absolute allegiance and obedience—as that of a slave who has but one purpose in life. This person is dominated by his or her master and lives to serve them.

It's curious, though, that Jesus chose money, of all the things He might have chosen, to be the counterpoint to God, isn't it? He didn't say, "You cannot serve both God and sex." Nor did He say, "You cannot serve both God and your job." He chose money, and this confirms that money indeed is the truest gauge of what we love.

That's actually very helpful for us because love is a tricky thing. Because the human heart is so complicated and so marred by sin, it's often difficult to know what it is that we actually love. Not what we say we love, because we are very proficient at making those kinds of noble announcements. But down deep inside, passed all the grandiose claims, what is truly at the center of our affection? That's a bit more difficult to diagnose.

Or maybe not.

According to Jesus, money is the primary competitor to God in our hearts. Perhaps that's because money is the means by which we might have any of these other elements. Power, sex, material goods—these all are funded and fueled by money. The old saying in police work is applicable in matters of the heart as well—follow the money trail. That's what Jesus is saying here. Follow the money and you get to the heart.

If you want to know—to really know—what you love, then take a brief survey of the last several months of your expenditures, and you might just come to an uncomfortable truth. Your money will show you your heart, and that is what God is interested in. The greatest commandment is about our heart, that we are to love God and love others, and all the rest of the commandments are summed up in that single statement.

Money is profoundly significant because it is the most sure way for us to know whether or not we love God and love others. Our bank accounts give us an accurate reading of our affections. But that's not all they show us. The way we treat money also reveals our faith.

Our Faith

Money shows us what we truly believe. In the same way that we might claim to love someone or something only to be disproven by our expenditures, we might make great claims about our faith only to have our bank accounts find us out. Think of the observation Jesus made upon seeing the example of a poor widow in the temple one day in Jerusalem:

> He looked up and saw the rich dropping their offerings into the temple treasury. He also saw a poor widow dropping in two tiny coins. "I tell you the truth," He said. "This poor widow has put in more than all of them. For all these people have put in gifts out of their surplus, but she out of her poverty has put in all she had to live on." (Luke 21:1–4)

Jesus wasn't very interested in counting the amount of giving that day in the temple. True, the rich gave much more. But Jesus looked deeper and ascribed value in more than dollars and cents. This woman was a widow, a station in life which would have put her primarily at the mercy of others' generosity. She was a woman of meager means, knowing that if she wasn't careful she would not have enough to live on. And yet she put in all she had, a sacrificial gift that deeply moved Jesus and caused His attention to be perked. Consider for a second what this woman must have believed to be true about God in order for her to treat her money in this way. Consider what her small coins revealed about her faith.

In order to treat her money in this fashion, she must have been firmly convinced of the goodness of God. She must have believed in His great ability to provide. She must have had an overwhelming trust in His character to motivate such a reckless financial decision. The way she treated her money was a window into what she believed to be true. The same thing applies to us, and can be most clearly seen in the common custom of tithing.

I say "custom" because people's opinions differ greatly on the subject. Some preach it as a Christian requirement; others paint it as more of a freewill offering. Some advocate for the generally accepted number of 10 percent; others see that as an unnecessary qualification that brings law where there should be grace. I'm not so much interested in the specific amount, as it seems that Jesus in this passage wasn't either. I'm more interested in the faith that motivates it. And faith does indeed motivate giving for us as well as it did the widow that day in the temple.

For the sake of argument, though, let's just say that you are a Christian who customarily gives to your church the first 10 percent of your paycheck. But then the economy goes south, or you acquire some unexpected medical bills. Or maybe you just take a hard look at the checkbook and realize how much more you could have socked away if you didn't give that full 10 percent. So you are tempted to cut back. You justify it by saying that it's not that you won't ever tithe again—you're just taking a few months off to get your feet under you. And isn't it sort of legalistic to have to write this check every month anyway? And doesn't God care about taking care of our families? That money could certainly be used to help them. Those are some of the things I have told myself, at least.

But all those excuses focus on a side issue. Tithing isn't really about the money. Just like most things in the Christian life, tithing has little to do with the actual, physical act and much more to do with the spiritual significance behind that act. Tithing has very little to do with money, and very much to do with faith. When we make the conscious choice to regularly and sacrificially give, we show that we aren't just giving lip service to God's power to provide and His goodness in doing so. Our faith is measured by our actions.

I believe that to continue to tithe—to be generous and giving even when you feel like you can't afford it—is an act of faith. It is a statement by action that I believe God can be trusted. He told me to do this, and so I will do it because I believe He is wise and loving in what He commands.

I will tithe also because I believe in God's power to provide. There's a lot that I could do with that money; and sometimes I feel like giving it away puts me in a position of need. That's not a position I'm comfortable with, but that is a position where I must receive from God. Not a bad place to be.

And I will tithe because I believe that God Himself is better than any of the stuff I could get with that money. It's an act of faith to choose God over comfort because, well, He's invisible. So I give away the money that could be used to make me more comfortable because I believe that God is better than any of those things.

We give because we trust. When we don't give, it's because we don't trust. Our wallets reveal, much more clearly than our words, the depth of our faith. Our faith is shown clearly in our common, ordinary expenditures.

Leave Margin

We cannot treat money casually. We cannot simply spend our way through life, one recurring bill at a time. We must not be bored by these matters of financial management, for these matters give us an accurate picture into our true love and faith. Ironically, one of the most helpful things we can do to bring intentionality to this boring area of our lives is through an equally boring tool: an intentionally generous budget. We can be active in making sure that our money is serving us and therefore serving God through making sure that we know where it's going. We cannot just *intend* to be generous but we must take active steps toward doing so.

One of the most challenging verses in the Bible to me in this respect is just dropped into Paul's practical instructions about life to the church at Ephesus: "The thief must no longer steal. Instead, he must do honest work with his own hands, so that he has something to share with anyone in need" (Eph. 4:28). Don't just stop stealing; start working. And don't just work to make money; make money so you have something to give. But let's take it a step further and say this: Make a boring, repeatable plan so that you can be sure you have enough to give. Write down how much you are going to spend on groceries, eating out, electricity, and gas, then cut where you need to so that you have enough to regularly practice generosity. It sounds boring I know, but through these small choices, we work out our love and our faith in God.

The Old Testament would articulate the principle like this: Don't plow to the edge of your field:

> "When you reap the harvest of your land, you are not to reap to the very edge of your field or gather the gleanings of your harvest. You must not strip your vineyard bare or gather its fallen grapes. Leave them for the poor and the foreign resident; I am Yahweh your God." (Lev. 19:9–10)

At first glance, these verses seems like one of those "throwaway" passages that New Testament Christians don't tend to pay a lot of attention to. We might lump it in with its neighboring commands about using the bathroom outside the camp and dealing with skin disorders. But there is much more going on here than might first be apparent. God is giving His people practical instruction to create margin in their lives. God is so concerned about the poor and the foreigners that He built in a means into the regular life of His people in order to provide food for them. He made sure that the people didn't harvest all the way to the edges of the field. The edges were "just in case."

Just in case someone traveling needs food.

Just in case you have the chance to share with someone who is in need.

Just in case someone else needs to feed their family.

Just in case the leftovers can be useful for something other than filling your own barns.

See it? This command defies the constant call of our culture for "more." It helps us to plan practically and regularly for generosity. It helps us exercise our love and faith, and we need that kind of intentionality because we live in a margin-less world. That's true not only in our finances; it's also true in our time. Our calendars are booked with meetings and appointments end to end. In fact, everything from our time to our money is pretty much spoken for. We are plowing to the end of the fields. We are going back over the fields of our lives a second and third time, looking for any spare cent or second that has not been accounted for.

The way you integrate this command into your real life today is that in all these areas, you don't plow to the edge. You don't book meetings back to back in case there is a conversation God will bring your way you need to have. You don't overschedule your family with activity after activity so that there isn't a single second to spend with your neighbors in the yard. And you certainly don't spend all the way to the end of your paycheck in case there is an unforeseen chance to be generous.

Once again, though, the impetus behind this margin is the constant gaze on Jesus. When you are looking to Him, you will find that all the imperatives of life don't seem quite so imperative any more. And suddenly those edges of the fields you thought you needed you find out can actually be set aside, creating room for intentional and regular generosity.

An ordinary life lived in light of the extraordinary God leaves that kind of room at the edges, just in case.

The truth is that we are all in debt to those who didn't plow to the edges of their fields. Somewhere, at some point, someone has given sacrificially for our sakes. They have lent us an ear when we desperately needed a conversation. They have made time when they could have counted us as unimportant. And yes, they have given us the money when there was not enough to go around. And then, of course, there's the most literal example of all.

During some dark days of Israel, days of great idolatry, there was still a man who took seriously the law of God and didn't plow to the edges. Because he didn't, a young widow named Ruth was able to glean the wheat from the edges in order to provide food for her and her mother-in-law, Naomi. Boaz, the owner of the field, ended up marrying the gleaner Ruth, and a few generations later Jesus Christ enters the world.

Great things can happen when you don't plow to the edges of your life. Ultimately, faith alone can drive you to such a choice, because you are consciously making an effort to choose less, even though you may not know the reason why. But what is "just in case" to us has divine meaning and purpose to God.

We should care about money. We should look carefully at the boring stuff of finances. It should matter to us as it matters to God, for it's through these common, everyday occurrences that we find out who we truly love and what we truly believe.

CHAPTER 9

NOSE TO THE GRINDSTONE

Working for the Weekend

My first job was pretty typical: I mowed grass all summer for a guy in my town with a lawn care business. It wasn't a great decision for a kid who suffered from allergies, but it did put a little money in my pocket for a while. At least I had something to use to buy Kleenex.

That's pretty much what that first job was—it was a means to an end. The means was pushing a lawn mower for eight hours a day; the end was money. I felt no great calling to agricultural engineering; nor did I sense the presence of the extraordinary in the Weed Eater string. I just showed up, day after day, doing the same thing as I did the previous day, and then got a check on Friday. For most of us, that's the same way we still approach work.

Work is a means to an end.

Work is something that's necessary, but not something particularly desirable. There are indeed the 2 percent of people out there who are doing what they love and jump out of bed every morning like they've been lying on a spring. God bless them. The rest of us, at least part of the time, have to take a deep breath over a cup of morning coffee to go back and do the same thing today that we did yesterday. For the rest of us, we tend to work not as an end in itself, but to get to do something else.

We work to go on vacation. We work for the weekend. We work so that someday we don't have to work any more. In other words, we work in order to be at leisure. We might be tempted to think the solution to work dissatisfaction is to get a new job. To be fair, that might indeed be what needs to happen. But if that's your perspective now, in the job you're currently in, chances are at some point in the future you'll have that perspective again.

If we find ourselves simply existing through the

workday in order to get to the weekend, then a deeper problem is at play, and a deeper solution is needed. Amazingly, the perspective we're looking for isn't found in another job, but right in the middle of our boring workweeks. To find the solution, we need to once again go back to the beginning of time, and of Scripture. God didn't create work to bore us. To Him, work is sacred, whether that work is emptying trash or preaching a sermon. A. W. Tozer reminded us once that "It is not what a man does that determines whether his work is sacred or secular. It is why he does it." The sacredness of the opportunity is not about the work itself, but about our perspective of why we work at all.

The Sacredness of Work

"What do you do?"

When you meet someone for the first time, you exchange names and pleasantries, and then the question above is close behind: "What do you do?" It's logical that it should be the next question. When you look at the sheer amount of time that you spend working every week, especially when you weigh it against the time you spend doing anything else, you would naturally wonder what a new acquaintance does with the bulk of his or her life. With the rise of technology, that amount of working time is being multiplied greatly.

Work e-mail is accessible at the touch of a button. Your cell phone is always in your pocket or purse. Gone are the days when you simply left the office. If you find yourself in a professional environment, you are constantly connected to your job because you are constantly connected to technology. In a way, it puts people in the office in the same situation as the people who work inside the home; it's not like a stay-at-home mom clocks out for the day. She's always on call, regardless of the day or night.

Whatever our jobs are, most work is cyclical in nature. You pretty much know what to expect after you leave the house in the morning or when the children wake up. You know that your day is going to be filled with the same requirements, the same obligations, and pretty much the same actions that it was filled with yesterday. Sure, there's an interruption every once in a while, but by and large it's going to be the same. Maybe that's why, when we get asked what we do, we reply with some kind of ambiguous job title meant to summarize all those tediously endless and cyclical actions:

"I'm a teacher."

"I'm a manager."

"I'm in sales."

Those things might be true, but they're rather non-specific. If we actually answered what we did, because that was the question, we'd have to say something like: "Well, I answer anywhere from forty to seventy-five e-mails a day and have meetings that take about two hours on average. I complete and sign expense reports and make sure shipments go out on time. I mop and sweep the floors after the restaurant closes down." You can insert anything that's applicable here; whatever it looks like, it's probably going to look much like that tomorrow too.

Boring, right?

Absolutely. It's a continual stream of the same activity day in and day out with very little variance. So if the answer isn't necessarily a change in vocation, what is it? It is possible, as C. S. Lewis said, to have "the sense of divine vision restored to man's daily work." What we might need instead of a change in vocation is a change in perspective, not just about our particular job, but about the nature of work in general.

Work is a sacred opportunity given to us by and for God, just as it was given to Adam on the very first day human beings walked on the earth. The day in question is recorded for us in Genesis 2. Think back to those quiet days of peace and harmony as God created the garden of Eden:

> These are the records of the heavens and the
> earth, concerning their creation at the time
> that the LORD God made the earth and the
> heavens. No shrub of the field had yet grown
> on the land, and no plant of the field had yet
> sprouted, for the LORD God had not made it

rain on the land, and there was no man to
work the ground. (Gen. 2:4–5)

These were early days. Days before it rained. Days
before shrubs and plants grew. But even in those early
days, God was thinking about work. He was going to
create man, according to verse 5, with the specific
intent that he would work the ground. The record continues in verse 15: "The LORD God took the man and
placed him in the garden of Eden to work it and watch
over it."

The pictures in children's Bibles of those early days,
complete with carefully placed plant life over certain
parts of the humans, might cause us to think that life
in the garden for Adam and Eve was some kind of pre-
sin picnic. We imagine the first humans spending their
days lounging under shade trees, eating berries off
bushes, and naming an animal here and there. That's
not what this text leads us to believe.

What we have here instead is a picture of God creating and positioning His children and then immediately
giving them a job. Just as God had been busy working,
so would the man, created in God's image, have work
ingrained in his DNA. That's right, friends—much as
we might view our jobs as only the means to the end
for our leisure, we were created to work. But we were
created to work with the right perspective.

The Hebrew word translated as *placed* literally
means "caused to rest." But that's a problem because it

seems, at least on the surface, to contradict God's command to man. How could the man be caused to rest and then given a job? The reason we fail to see this reveals just how misshapen our view of work has become.

For Adam, work was not opposed to rest. It was not a necessary evil only done to earn money and play on the weekend. Instead, work was a blessing, born out of the sense of rest he had through his relationship with God. This is the first point in our perspective that must be changed.

Most of us find our primary identity and self-worth in what we do for a living. We are doctors, lawyers, teachers, writers, or whatever. When we are asked that question, "What do you do?" we internally translate it to mean, "Who are you? What worth do you have? What do you contribute?" Our jobs are the means by which others see us and the means by which we see ourselves.

We must understand that what goes on a business card is not the summation of our identity. Adam had that kind of different perspective. Adam lived in an unbroken and unmarred relationship with God; his identity was secure in that relationship. He was completely and fully satisfied in God; there was no sense of having to prove himself and validate his worth. He was confident in God's love and care and, because he was, his work was able to flow from that security. It was that perspective that allowed him to see work not as a curse but a blessing, not something that contradicted resting but something that rose out of it.

Adam didn't work to earn respect or validation; he worked because he wanted to do so, for he knew who God was and who he was in God. He was created to work. But then came the fall of man in Genesis 3, and everything changed, including our perspective on work.

The Corruption of Work

In those same children's Bibles, we see pictures of a man and a woman hiding from God, ashamed of their nakedness. We see them exiled from the garden as their single choice threw the entire created order into chaos. We see that unbroken freedom and fellowship with God now marred by sin and the advent of the guilt and shame that comes along with it. From that point on, we, as the children of Adam, are members of the rebellion against the loving reign of God instigated by their choice. Sin is more than just a series of bad choices; it's a condition in which we find ourselves. Everything in our world is influenced by sin. That includes things like our propensity to make bad choices, but it also includes things that might not be so readily apparent. Earthquakes, hurricanes, and cancer are all a part of this distorted order, all finding their ultimate root in a universe that has been thrown off-kilter by sin.

The sacredness of our work has also been corrupted by sin. In fact, the effect of sin on work is one of the things God articulated as a direct consequence of the fall:

> "The ground is cursed because of you. You will
> eat from it by means of painful labor all the
> days of your life. It will produce thorns and
> thistles for you, and you will eat the plants
> of the field. You will eat bread by the sweat
> of your brow until you return to the ground,
> since you were taken from it. For you are dust,
> and you will return to dust." (Gen. 3:17–19)

After the fall, work changed. What once was a blessing became a curse. What once was a joy became a trial. What once was freedom became strained. That's what we are living in the middle of, and that's part of the reason we look at work with resentment.

Unlike Adam in those early days, we don't work because we are accepted; we work to gain acceptance. We work not because we are justified but to justify ourselves. We work not because we are loved but because we worry we are not. Because we do not have the firm confidence that comes with right standing with God, we look to other things to fill the gaping void of our identity. We don't know who we are, and one of the easiest places to look to find that out is to the very thing that occupies so much of our time—our jobs.

But this perspective, along with everything else, changes in the gospel. Because of the gospel, we know that whatever we do in whatever vocation we find ourselves in, we are fully accepted on the merit and righteousness of Jesus alone. The gospel frees us from the burden of performance and self-justification and allows us to regain the sacred perspective of work. We no longer work primarily in order to establish or maintain our sense of identity; that's been taken care of in Christ. We know who we are, regardless of what our business cards say. We are the blood-bought and beloved children of God now and forevermore. Because we are, we can begin to see work as a blessing rather than a curse.

Like everything else in life, our perspective on work is dramatically and wonderfully redeemed when we begin to accept that we are fully acceptable to God because of the sacrifice of Jesus. Once we know that we ultimately have nothing left to prove to God because Jesus has done all the proving for us, we can begin to see work as a blessing rather than drudgery. When we begin to realize just how secure we are in Christ—that He has determined once for all our worth and significance—we no longer have to look to our job to determine our self-worth and our identity. This doesn't actually diminish the importance of work; it moves it into its proper sphere. Work then becomes one of the primary ways that we honor God.

Work and Worship

Two terms are used in Genesis 2:15 to describe the job God gave to Adam: "The LORD God took the man and placed him in the garden of Eden to work it and watch over it." In the Old Testament, the words *work* and *watch over* are most frequently used in discussions of human service to God, rather than describing a farmer's job. Surprisingly, these words are often connected to worship, or even the actions of priests serving in the tabernacle of God.

If Adam had a business card, it would have read "Gardener." Nothing exciting there. And yet the words God used to describe his job are anything but ordinary. Perhaps, at least in God's mind, there isn't such a wide divide between those things as there is to us.

Think of it like this: God could have, if He wanted, filled the whole earth with human beings in the same way He fashioned Adam—from the dust of the ground. But rather than taking that approach, He looked on Adam and gave him and his wife the responsibility and privilege of populating the earth. It's still controlled, upheld, and blessed by God, but He chose in His sovereignty to use regular people as the means of establishing His intent on the earth. Work can be seen much in the same way. Through work, God is using regular, ordinary people as His means of providing for His creation.

As our perspective on work changes through the gospel, we begin to see that the menial tasks we find

ourselves involved in day in and day out are actually—and amazingly—infused with incredible meaning. They are the sovereignly designed means by
which God is caring for the people of the earth. He has
ordained that we, as human beings, exist in a state of
interdependence on each other. That doesn't mean God
has isolated Himself from the world; it simply means
that God is providentially using the talents, opportunities, and regular old jobs of regular old people to provide and care for humanity.

Think of that. As we work, we are the means of
God. We become like the rain that falls on the just and
unjust alike—the means of common grace through
which human life and well-being is sustained and
provided for. When we see it like that, a sense of great
wonder and awe returns to our everyday working life,
for we come to see that God is channeling His love
through us as we work. He doesn't just work through
people involved in service industries, whose mission statements are written to benefit mankind. He
channels His love through the man who collects the
garbage on the streets early in the morning so that a
community can be clean and free of disease. It happens through the farmer who raises crops that can be
turned into clothes to keep children warm. It happens,
as Martin Luther said during his time, even through
the most humble functions and stations of life: God
Himself is milking the cows through the vocation

of the milkmaid. Centuries later, Luther's namesake Martin Luther King Jr. would say something similar: "All labor that uplifts humanity has dignity and importance and should be undertaken with painstaking excellence."[3]

Not only should we look at our own jobs with a renewed sense of awe as we are being used by God for the ultimate good of others; but every single job deserves our respect and gratitude. It's these common, everyday, run-of-the-mill jobs that channel the love of God and therefore are a sacred means of bringing great honor to Him. When you stop seeing your job as the means to a paycheck and start seeing it as a means of glorifying the providing God, it changes the way you flip burgers, change diapers, or put together a report.

Seeing work with this divine perspective isn't only liberating; it's also constraining. It makes you realign your thinking and examine your purposes. It forces you to examine whether you are indeed working with God and others in mind or whether you are simply socking away money until you can retire and move to Florida. It constrains the kind of career you have, forcing you to examine whether or not your job is a legitimate expression of the grace and care of God or whether your vocation is one bent on self-promotion and greed.

But it's through evaluating these issues that we actually return to the honor and sacredness of work. It is through this examination that we see the transcendent purpose God has for work, and that this purpose is found not necessarily through changing jobs, but through renewing your perspective right where you are.

You Are Called

Calling is a spiritual-sounding word that's often only reserved for those professional Christians who make their living by working for a church or a missions organization. But if what we've said above is true, we must also see that the word *calling* is just as applicable to the mom as it is to the preacher. This is actually more than semantics. When we use the word, we are expressing our belief that we don't just happen to find ourselves in this station or that one; we are showing that we truly believe in God's intricate involvement and positioning, that He has put us in this particular position for this particular time. Though we might have ambitions of a different job (and there's nothing wrong with that), we are embracing the fact that, no matter how humble the role, God has put us in that job for this moment.

Paul articulated the perspective like this in Colossians 3:23–24: "Whatever you do, do it enthusiastically, as something done for the Lord and not for men, knowing that you will receive the reward of an inheritance from the Lord. You serve the Lord Christ."

It's a simple articulation of a profoundly transformative principle—that what we are doing at any given moment can be done enthusiastically and with joy because ultimately we are not doing those things for men. We are doing them for the Lord.

We aren't just earning paychecks.

We aren't just saving up for retirement and vacation.

We aren't just pining away at some thankless task.

We are engaged in something holy. In something sacred. In something with great meaning, whether that something involves flipping burgers or balancing budgets. It is holy because we have a renewed perspective on it thanks to the gospel. And we are beginning to see the dignity, honor, and yes, even worship that is part of just another day at the office. God has uniquely positioned us, at least for a season, that we might be the means by which He extends His great grace to the whole of humanity.

In fact, it's through some of the most thankless jobs that we see the love and care of God most tangibly displayed. Not long ago, my family and I were wolfing down chicken sandwiches and nuggets in an attempt to get to the indoor playland in the corner of the restaurant as quickly as possible. And as the last bits of French fries were going down, one of the employees walked over to the trash can next to our table. As he was emptying the trash, my son, in a loud voice that only an eight-year-old can manage, announced that he would never want to have a job like that.

I understand where he's coming from. I'm not looking to trade careers at this point either. But what he, and I, need to understand is that there is great honor in what that man was doing while we were enjoying our dinner. Indeed, one of the reasons we could enjoy our dinner is because that person was willing to empty that trash. He was, in fact, a channel of God's common grace to our family; it was because of his job that I could sit and enjoy a dinner with my family.

Thank God for him.

And while we're on the subject of respect, I have to admit that I don't know that person's story. I don't know what brought him to that particular career. Perhaps it's a part-time gig for him, something he was doing to earn money for college or graduate school. But maybe he has a family too. Maybe his family was at home in an apartment or small house, and that job for him is the means by which he is keeping the lights on for his wife and children.

I don't know, and that's the point. I don't have to know in order to see the honor, glory, and presence of God in good, hard work. You are called, mom. You are called, teacher. You are called, accountant. You are called. The question is whether or not you know and believe it.

CHAPTER 10

SAME OLD SUNDAY

Sunday Morning

Let me paint the picture for you. It's a crisp morning with a slight layer of dew on the newly mowed grass outside. The birds are chirping; you gently awake. You lounge for a few minutes, grateful for the temporary quietness of the house. You walk outside in your pajamas to get the paper, the one time a week it comes. You walk back inside to sit for a few minutes and enjoy a little coffee, but you know that the relative peace of the moment is going to end.

Because this is Sunday.

So begins, if you have small children, the weekly ritual of getting the kids out of bed, getting them dressed, combing the snot and toothpaste out of their hair, braiding said hair, rushing out the door as you wonder to yourself, *Why do they take so long to get ready for church? They never take this long to get ready for school.*

Then, depending on the specific style and culture of your church, comes the settling in together in the chairs or pews. You steel your nerves for the coming effort that it's going to take to remind your children to be still and quiet, to wipe the drool from the sleeping child off your pants, and to draw the picture on the worship bulletin for them to color. Once your brood reassembles after worship and gets in the car to head home, one word throbs over and over in your head:

Nap.

Or something like that.

If you have currently or have had young children, you can probably resonate with some part of the routine. No doubt it takes effort to get up and get out the door. It takes perseverance and patience to explain, again, to the kids the necessity of being in church as a family. But perhaps, amidst the whining voices saying, "This is boring!" there is the thought, somewhere in the back of your mind, that simply wonders whether this whole routine is really worth it or not.

You're not alone.

I Like Jesus, But . . .

The vast majority of churches in North America have either plateaued or are declining in their membership. That's not to say that people aren't interested in spiritual things—even explicitly "Christian" spiritual things. But the church is no longer seen as essential to people's spiritual quests and development. Increasingly, people claim to like Jesus but not care too much for the church. To them, the church is an institution—"the man"—something that impedes spirituality rather than encourages it. They see the church as a place that teaches rules and behaviorism but cares little about its community and the rest of the world.

People with this view may have a point. The truth is that there is some validity to a few of those arguments. Churches have certainly, on occasion, gone their own way, pushed their own agenda, and failed to live up to their biblical calling. They also, as does any organization, have the tendency to become ingrown and self-focused to the detriment of their surroundings. While those charges come primarily from people outside the doors of churches, I've got to wonder, whether those of us who do show up, week after week, still think on occasion, *What are we doing here? Are we just singing songs? Why are we going through the effort to keep showing up, week after week? What is this thing of which we're supposed to be a part?*

That language of "supposed to" really hits home with me. Most of us would acknowledge that going to church is a positive thing, and yet very few of us can articulate why. We come, in the end, because we think we are supposed to. The problem is that "supposed to" will only get you so far. "Supposed to" doesn't help much when the schedule gets busy. "Supposed to" doesn't motivate when the kids start to roll their eyes on Sunday mornings. "Supposed to" doesn't get you out the door when you start thinking that your preacher isn't exciting enough or that the worship isn't engaging enough.

If there's no deeper reason to come to church, then we will follow the trend we see throughout Christianity when families jump from church to church, like people searching for a the latest local restaurant to try, each time looking for one that is more exciting. More challenging. More engaging. More to their liking. Until they stop coming altogether.

An Individual Faith?

Part of the problem comes naturally to us. We do, after all, live in a primarily individualistic culture, and that individualism has infiltrated Christianity. One way we see this individuality is in our language.

There is one key phrase that we, as Christians, like to use when talking about our faith. We like to talk about having a "personal relationship with Jesus Christ." I get why we say that; it emphasizes that we have more than a casual acquaintanceship with Jesus. We have a relationship, and like any relationship, it can be deep or shallow. It needs to be nurtured. We also find that the relationship is personal. We don't enter into it because of our association with a group or because we have a membership card. We come into it because something has happened to us individually, as persons. But here's the interesting thing: When the Bible describes how we interact with Jesus, we don't find the term "personal relationship with Christ" anywhere in its pages. Sure, the ideas are there, but the terminology is absent. Terminology like that is neither helpful nor biblical, for it increases our already present tendency to isolate our experiences with God. We are rugged individualists, and like any good Americans, we believe that we can do anything ourselves. Anything worth doing is worth doing alone, for being on a team is really a sign of weakness.

So if that terminology isn't there in Scripture, what is there? Among other things, scores of verses emphasize that though we might have been individually called out of darkness into light, we weren't the only individuals who have been called. We have come into the people of God. That is the church. Discovering the answer to that fundamental question of what we are really doing in the church will fuel our resolve not to consume the church but to love her. Not to take from the church but to give. And not to abandon the church but to keep coming back, over and over again.

What Is the Church?

The Bible talks about the church not as a place you go, but as a people you are. That's what the church literally is—the *ekklesia*, the "called out ones." Not a building. Not an institution. A people. A family. The Bible considers the church as God's means to reach the world. Not aid organizations. Not governments. Not even individuals. The church is God's Plan A. And there is no Plan B.

The Bible also describes the church as both the body and the bride of Christ. The "body" is more than just a metaphor. Because the Holy Spirit of God literally indwells the hearts of believers, we become the body of Christ, moving throughout the world to accomplish His good purposes and will. And as the bride of Christ, we are the beloved and betrothed. Those metaphors make the "you can be just fine as a Christian who likes Jesus but who hates the church" idea absolutely ludicrous.

Let's say that, after you read this book, you are kind enough to drop me a note that says something like, "Michael, thanks for taking the time to write this book. I really enjoyed reading it, and genuinely wasn't bored too often. And I think I would even like you as a person. You don't seem like a huge jerk. But when you talk about your wife? Man, I'm glad I've never met her. She sounds awful."

Not a great opening set of remarks. I take it as a personal offense when you insult my wife because we are joined together as one. Insult her, and you insult me too. When we say we like Jesus but not the church, we are saying that we hate His wife. Are we really ready to tell Him that?

In addition, the bulk of the New Testament was written not to individuals but to specific churches; its letters were meant to be read and understood in the context of the community of God's people. The church is extremely important to God. It's not optional. But let's be honest: does knowing that it's not meant to be an option really help make church more exciting? It might help with the commitment level and resolve, but it doesn't do a lot to help us see the great and extraordinary significance in the middle of the sermons, the songs, and the passing of the offering plates. To that end, there is something else that we need to see. Something that shows us an amazing upward glimpse into the cosmic and universal significance of the church. Something that propels us past elementary discussions of worship style and preacher rhetoric. That something comes to us from Ephesians 3.

The Church on Display

The book of Ephesians has much to say about individuals. You find some great Scripture in there that talks about what God does in the life of every person who has become a Christ follower. In Ephesians 2, for example, Paul reminds us that before Christ, we were dead in our sin, without hope or chance, absolutely lost. But God, in His grace, made us alive in Christ, not because of what we have done, but because of His work on the cross.

Death to life. That's the gospel. And I suppose Paul could have stopped there. It's a fine summation and explanation of the gospel. But the gospel doesn't stop at the individual level. It didn't for the Ephesian believers and it certainly doesn't for us.

The specific problem in Ephesus that Paul was addressing was that these people—these individuals who once were dead but then made alive in Christ—were having trouble understanding how they fit together. They were a culturally and ethnically diverse congregation, made up of spiritually resurrected people from various countries around the world. Arguing, backbiting, selfishness, and opinions were running rampant in their midst. Paul could have said, "You guys need to just remember what happened when you came to know Christ. Sure, it's great if you meet together, but let's not complicate the issue. From this point forward, we are going to have Jewish worship at 8 a.m. We'll have rams' horns blowing and the Scripture read in Hebrew. But you need to be out of the building by 10, because that's when the Greek worship service starts, and they're going to be eating ham sandwiches at the potluck after lunch, and you certainly don't want to be around for that."

Paul didn't say that.

For him, it was absolutely essential that these Ephesian believers come together and form one church out of many individuals. Paul understood that the gospel doesn't just reconcile man to God, it reconciles man to man. That's why in the next verses he wrote about how in Christ, we are made into one new person—the church. He elaborated on how the death of Christ has torn down the dividing wall of hostility between ethnic groups in order that they come together as one. For Paul, it was absolutely imperative that these people—these diverse individuals—come together to form one single body in the church though it certainly would have been easier for him to keep them separated, each according to their culture and preference.

He was so insistent they come together because in the church, there is a much, much deeper level of reality going on than what meets the eye. This greater reality is happening right in the middle of the ordinary people, singing in their off-key kind of way, trying to wrangle their ornery children. In the middle of the mundane there is something of cosmic significance going on.

As in all the other areas of everyday life we've considered, there is the physical level of reality and the spiritual level of reality. Each is ongoing, and each is just as real as the other. Everything we see and experience, we see and experience at the physical level of reality. That includes the rustling of the trees in the wind, the way we interact with our girlfriends and boyfriends and eventually spouses, and even what and how we eat. But at the same time that all this stuff is happening at a physical level of reality, there is a greater—and even deeper—level of reality going on. We're not aware of it many times, but becoming increasingly aware of the spiritual is how these boring areas of life are transformed into something more.

A regular life isn't just a series of physical times and moment strung together; it's a progression of being formed into the image of Jesus. A casual conversation isn't just a series of words between friends; it's an interaction between beings made in the image of God. A marriage isn't just a contract between two people; it's a walking, talking illustration of the reality of the gospel. Parenting isn't just teaching kids to be good citizens; it's seeing our children as arrows of light shot into darkness. And finances aren't just a few bucks here and there; they are the window into what we love and what we believe.

See it? Two levels of reality, and the same thing is happening in the case of the church. At the base level of reality, we might say that it's important to be a part of the church because it enhances spiritual growth. Or because it provides an opportunity to serve. Or because it provides an avenue for corporate worship, accountability, receiving of teaching, or any number of very important things. But there is a greater level of reality going on here too, and we find Paul articulating the greater level of reality in Ephesians 3:7–11:

> I was made a servant of this gospel by the gift
> of God's grace that was given to me by the
> working of His power. This grace was given
> to me—the least of all the saints—to proclaim
> to the Gentiles the incalculable riches of the
> Messiah, and to shed light for all about the
> administration of the mystery hidden for
> ages in God who created all things. This is so
> God's multi-faceted wisdom may now be made
> known through the church to the rulers and
> authorities in the heavens. This is according
> to His eternal purpose accomplished in the
> Messiah, Jesus our Lord.

This greater level of reality prevented Paul from taking the pragmatic approach of splitting up different ethnic groups. Their unity was much more important than just getting along with each other at worship

183

services and in the community because in the church, God is revealing His glorious wisdom and power. The church is where these attributes of God are put on display. God has chosen to reveal His great character through you and me, as we give ourselves to our regular, local church.

Even more amazing is the fact that God isn't just using the church as His revelation on earth; He's making Himself known to the rulers and authorities in the heavenly realms. That means the church has a cosmic, universal purpose that is a bigger extension of its purpose here on earth. It's as if God has put the church on a shelf in front of the entire world—and even more than the world, in front of all of the heavenly powers as a display of His glory. It's as if God is saying to the universe, "Do you want to know about Me? Do you want to know about My wisdom? My power? My grace? Are these things only ethereal concepts to you? Well, not any more. Take a look here, and you'll see what My character looks like." We are on display to the heavenlies.

Consider, for a moment, what a church unified in its experience of the gospel displays to the cosmos. Nowhere else do we find people of such a rich diversity in culture, language, income, education, and status coming together. Surely whatever brings people like this—people who would have no cause or commonality between them—must be awesome. Something like this could only be the work of God done in order to display the greatness of His wisdom, grace, and power.

God did not choose the stars for this purpose. He didn't choose the intricate design of the atom or the creative look of the kangaroo. He doesn't hold up the vast expanse of the oceans or the limitless bounds of space. He chose the church, filled with the regular, ordinary, boring people we rub shoulders with every weekend. Church is more than singing a few songs and listening to a talk here and there. Through the church, we are a part of the revelation of the wisdom of God. Glorious.

A Group Project

This revelation that's happening in the church includes you and me. If we choose to be the people who treat the church like a disposable entity to be consumed until we can find something exciting to us, then we are robbing the church of an essential piece of what she needs to fulfill her purpose: us.

Consider Paul's words in Romans 12:1–2:

Therefore, brothers, by the mercies of God,
I urge you to present your bodies as a living
sacrifice, holy and pleasing to God; this is your
spiritual worship. Do not be conformed to this
age, but be transformed by the renewing of

your mind, so that you may discern what is the good, pleasing, and perfect will of God.

I know, I know—these verses don't look like they're about the church. But look a little deeper. Specifically, take a look at whether the words in verse 1 are singular or plural. There's some of each, right? *Brothers*—plural. Sure. This isn't a letter written to an individual, but to a group, meant to be read, understood, and obeyed in that community context. *Mercies*—plural. No doubt there. God's mercies are innumerable, and Paul has spent the previous eleven chapters articulating them. "Bodies"—plural again. Many brothers, many bodies. That makes sense.

But then we come to this word: "sacrifice." That's singular. So what we see here is Paul, writing to a church, telling them that they are, in their many bodies, to come together and offer one corporate sacrifice. We usually treat this verse in an individualistic context. You have to make the choice about your body, whether or not you will offer yourself to God as a living sacrifice. We think of it as a "me and God" issue, that every morning I have the choice about whether or not to crawl up on the altar and offer myself for God's purposes that day.

While that's certainly a biblical notion, it's not primarily what Paul is talking about here. The fact that "sacrifice" is singular propels this passage from an individual project to a group project: many bodies, only one sacrifice.

Now if you're like me, that's not particularly great news. I've always hated group projects. I've heard all the arguments why working in groups is a great idea, both from teachers and from students. Teachers will say that it's in groups where students learn how to group problem-solve and to develop skills essential for working with others; students will agree that the program is great because there is not so much pressure on them—it is more evenly distributed. An added bonus is that each student doesn't have to do as much work—it's spread out among many. I don't care. I don't like group projects because you can't trust people! How do you know that he is going to type the report, that she is going to do the PowerPoint presentation, and that she is going to do the background research? You don't! Too bad for me, though, because that's just what Paul is describing here.

Not only that, but he is saying that this group project is God's will for our lives as Christians. Not much wiggle room there. Far from an individualistic sacrifice, the picture here is for each member of the church to link arms with each other member and for all of them to crawl up on the altar together. Many bodies; only one sacrifice that is holy and pleasing to God. It is in that moment of collective offering of ourselves as one, unified sacrifice that we will be able to test and approve what God's good, pleasing, and perfect will is.

But even there Paul is not content; he goes on and defines what God's will is:

> For by the grace given to me, I tell every-
> one among you not to think of himself more
> highly than he should think. Instead, think
> sensibly, as God has distributed a measure of
> faith to each one. Now as we have many parts
> in one body, and all the parts do not have the
> same function, in the same way we who are
> many are one body in Christ and individu-
> ally members of one another. According to the
> grace given to us, we have different gifts: If
> prophecy, use it according to the standard of
> one's faith; if service, in service; if teaching, in
> teaching; if exhorting, in exhortation; giving,
> with generosity; leading, with diligence; show-
> ing mercy, with cheerfulness. (Rom. 12:3–8)

The way you participate in that group sacrifice is by doing what you have been created to do for the sake of the church. Everything in your life—your upbring-ing, your experiences, your physical appearance, your talents, your giftings from the Holy Spirit—these things have not happened by chance. You have been formed very specifically. It is when you minister in the way that God created you to that you are most satisfied and effective. And yet, you are not to try to do everything.

His desire is that you come to understand specifically who you have been formed and made to be in Christ.

Let the preachers preach. Let the servers serve. Let the merciful have mercy. You are not made to do everything. This is what he means when he says that each one should have a sober—a realistic—estimation of him or herself.

When we know who God has made us to be and accept that person, we look around and see that in the midst of our diversity we are coming together. An arm here, a leg there—and the body of Christ is beginning to form. Each person comfortable in their own skin, abilities, and role, no one more important than the other, all linked together so that when one part suffers they all feel it, and all working together for the same goal. This is the living sacrifice that we are to offer—to be the body of Christ. But the church cannot be the church, cosmically revealing the great wisdom of God, unless you are willing to be you.

Don't Rob the Church

Let me say it again: The church cannot be the church unless you are willing to be you. This can be gloriously freeing, or terribly crushing. It's liberating to think of playing an essential role in this cosmic purpose, a role that fits in line with who you were formed and created to be. The Lord is not asking you to preach!

The Lord is not asking you to prophesy! He is asking you to be yourself—no one else. What amazing freedom. Surely this is good news, unless, of course, it's the worst news possible. And indeed it might be.

It's not good news for the businessman who cheats on his wife after twenty years of marriage because he is bored with his white-collar life. It's not good news for the stay-at-home mom who loses herself in romance novels every day because she resents so much that her life revolves around her children. It's not good news for the person with the eating disorder who can't understand why the diet never works.

We are too fat, too thin, too smart, too dumb, too funny, too loud, too quiet, too introverted, or too extroverted, and so this truth about the church might not be good news for us at all. If the church being the church is dependent on me being me, than nothing could be worse, and you know why just as I do—because we don't like who we are. We hate ourselves.

This kind of self-loathing has no place in the church. It's not that we bring an arrogance with us to this group sacrifice, but it is that we recognize our intrinsic value to the body of Christ. These regular churchgoers are sons and daughters of the living God, who looks at all of us and with tears in His eyes, says, "I am proud to be called your Father." They are the perfect righteousness of Christ. They are an essential part of his body, without whom we are all somehow incomplete. They are uniquely formed and gifted human beings that are fearfully and wonderfully made. We recognize all these things because that is what the Lord sees.

When we have a sober and accurate estimation of ourselves, then we follow in the long line of saints that have gone before us who also have sober estimations of themselves. We follow in the footsteps of Moses who knew that he could hear God's voice but could not speak it, and so Aaron became his mouthpiece. We follow in the line of Abraham who had faith that could move mountains, and yet he knew that he was not a priest and so he brought his sacrifice to Melchizidek. We follow in the line of David who knew that though he could defeat one giant he could not defeat the entire army, so he surrounded himself with mighty men. Or men like Peter who was a great evangelist to the Jews, but knew he was not best equipped to reach the Gentiles and so he commissioned Paul. Or Paul himself who had the greatest theological mind the world has ever known, and yet he accepted support from the church at Philippi.

This is what the Lord loves—diversity operating in unity, each person as himself, but people freely giving themselves for the great purpose of God in the church. We're not just called to get together and sing a few songs. It's more than that, but the "more" is accomplished not outside of the ordinary life of the church but right in the middle. We begin to see it when we give ourselves willingly to God's great purposes that include us—as ordinary we might be.

CHAPTER 11

RISE AND STAND

Let me tell you another story if I could. This one is very much like the story on the first page of this book, and yet very different all at the same time. It's a story about that same ordinary person, doing the same ordinary things. It's a story filled with the same details: the same alarm clock still goes off. The same eggs have to be made every morning. The same commute still has to be driven. The same homework has to be done with the same children, and the same wife still sleeps on the same side of the bed.

It's all the same, and yet it's all different because those same events are suddenly viewed through an entirely new set of lenses. See, that ordinary, run-of-the-mill person has come to understand that the presence of God isn't constrained to the big and exciting—He invades the seemingly small and mundane details of life too. Because an extraordinary and active God is there, constantly working, there is no such thing as ordinary anymore.

It's not an ordinary marriage.

It's not just a couple of dollars.

It's not the same old parenting struggles.

It's not another day at the office.

Everything is the same, but everything is suddenly very different. That's what this book has been about—not escaping the ordinary, but reshaping our view of the ordinary in light of the extraordinary God. I hope this book, by God's grace, has helped you take a step toward removing the word "just" from your vocabulary: You're not just a mom. You're not just a teacher. You're not just a student, just a taxpayer, or just a church member. No one is who follows an extraordinary God.

Loaves, Fish, and Unself-conscious Little Boys

Maybe, by God's grace, you've captured a vision over these several pages of what it might look like to, as Brother Lawrence once said, practice the presence of God in both the big and small. To become cognizant of the great presence and purpose of God in the mundane and ordinary. Not to escape, but to live a life of faithfulness in these details. Maybe the partition between the sacred and secular is beginning to crack.

But maybe, if you're like me, something is still in the way. As much as you don't want to think of yourself as "just-a-whatever," the nagging feeling is still inside you that even if you do believe all this stuff, it doesn't really change anything. You might begin to see the extraordinary in daily life for a little while, but you know that after about a week you're back to talking yourself into something that's not really there.

It's going to feel like you're convincing yourself that you like coffee because that's what all the cool people like, even though you know in your heart that you don't. Jesus has something to say about that kind of thing. It's a statement that forces us to take our eyes off of our boring circumstances and instead put them on the extraordinary God we follow. It's an exhortation that urges us to lose ourselves in wonder rather than find ourselves in the midst of the mundane. A long time ago, Jesus said that if we want to come into the kingdom of God, we must become like little children (Mark 10:15).

As a dad of three young kids, this stirs my soul. When I look at them and see the way they see the world, I long for simplicity and trust. Of self-forgetfulness and joy. It makes me think of the picture of Jabba the Hut that I have on the wall of my office.

Joshua, my now eight-year-old, colored it for me when he was four. I like to look at it sometimes, but not because it's a technically awesome picture. Everybody knows that Jabba is brown—not green. And I think even Jabba himself might be offended at how liberally the crayon goes outside the lines. Furthermore, Joshua's message at the top of the paper, "I LOV YOU," is misspelled.

But I love that picture, and it will hang in my office for some time. The eight-year-old Joshua wouldn't present me with such a picture, because now he would deem such a creation as unworthy of his skills. His internal monologue has changed. It once was, "My daddy will love this. He will be so proud of me," but I fear it is becoming "I didn't do a very good job. I can do better. I can't give him something like this."

That makes me very sad.

I don't think this shift in thinking is because Joshua is being raised in an environment where he has to jockey for his parents' love and approval; by God's grace, we are generous with praise and he knows he is unconditionally loved. Instead, I believe it is the process that happens to all of us when we become more and more conscious of ourselves.

We care about our physical appearance more than we used to.

We notice how our voice sounds in comparison to others.

We, for the first time, start to wonder if we are actually "cool" or not.

You know the feeling. It's the one when you find yourself surrounded by people who work more interesting jobs, take more interesting vacations, and live generally more interesting lives. Suddenly, you find that you are shrinking into yourself, very conscious of your normality in light of what's surrounding you.

It's that sense of self-consciousness that Jesus speaks into. His advice is simple—become like a little child. Abandon that self-consciousness and instead find a renewed and simple sense of wonder. Revert back to innocence, to the days when we gladly gave our fathers those metaphorical pictures of Jabba the Hut with misspelled messages of affection. Here's a case study that might help.

Think about the miraculous lunch in John 6. The disciples faced a seemingly insurmountable issue, and they were at a loss. The people (at least 5,000 and probably twice that at least) were hungry. But, as the disciples so aptly put it to Jesus, it would take almost a year's salary to buy enough food to feed them (John 6:7).

Perhaps you remember the end of the story too. Jesus used the gift of a little boy—five barley loaves and two fish—to feed a multitude. It's a great story, but here's the thing: Are we to believe that this boy was the only one in the crowd who had remembered to pack a lunch for the day? Probably not. Surely there was a conscientious mother somewhere on the hill who had a package of crackers in her purse. So where were all the other volunteers?

We can't say for sure, for the Bible does not. Maybe their food was spoiled. Maybe they were selfish and didn't present it. Maybe this boy was simply the one closest to Andrew and so his lunch box got chosen. We don't know, but maybe . . .

Maybe the adults in the crowd had the same attitude as the disciples. They were self-conscious about the best they could do, so they kept their lunches to themselves. Maybe they looked at what they had to offer and were suddenly overcome by the overwhelming sense of normalcy: *This isn't enough. It's not even worth putting out there. I don't have anything valid to offer. Somebody's going to laugh at me if I walk up there carrying this.* Driven inward by their self-consciousness, they were paralyzed into inaction and silence.

We will likely have the same feeling as we seek to find the extraordinary in the midst of the ordinary. We will have a heart full of wonder, and yet at some point we will be tempted to look at our own boring potential and, like the self-conscious adults we are, just go about the business of life.

Part of following Jesus is overcoming that self-consciousness. It's coming to Jesus with all we have, small though it may be, and giving it to Him.

The real issue with self-consciousness is the "self" part. We're too busy thinking about our own weaknesses and inadequacies to consider the greatness of Jesus. Our focus is on ourselves rather than on the multiplier of fish.

I want to bring my badly colored pictures to God. My measly fish and broken bread. My weak faith and my inconstant prayer life. My normal routine of everyday stuff. I want to bring them to Him because I believe that the One I'm presenting them to is bigger than my weakness. Oh, to forget myself and be lost in the grandeur of Jesus. Oh, to regain the sense of wonder that characterizes little children who haven't yet grown into that self-conscious sense of foolishness. We must regain this sense of wonder that motivated a little boy to bring his normal, little lunch box to Jesus and see what happened. We must not be too grown up to believe. We must, in the end, focus our gaze on Jesus, for it's only in and through Him that we will see the boring issues of life suddenly be multiplied and transformed.

Faithfulness in an Age of Abandonment

What does that unswerving gaze on Jesus look like? What does it mean for an ordinary life? It means making one of the most difficult choices in an age when abandonment of the boring details of life is the norm. It means pursuing faithfulness, while everyone else is worshipping at the idols of more and excitement.

We find ourselves confronted, in this age, to search for that elusive "else." Another opportunity, another contract, more money, increased exposure, more notoriety, greater fame, and so on. Something other than what you've been given in life. If I'm honest, I think I spend a great deal of time either chasing after or fantasizing about that ever-elusive "else." Into that quest, the Lord speaks the word of faithfulness. Paul advised the church at Thessalonica to "seek to lead a quiet life, to mind your own business, and to work with your own hands, as we commanded you, so that you may walk properly in the presence of outsiders and not be dependent on anyone" (1 Thess. 4:11–12).

In other words, do your job, and do it with all your might as unto the Lord. Wash the dishes. Change the diapers. Prepare the spreadsheet. Parent the children. Attend the meeting. Do your job faithfully. Do not run away searching for something else out there; stay put. Stay faithful. Present your small, quiet, boring offering to the Lord unself-consciously, and wait to see what happens. It's not big; it's not necessarily exciting. But built into that faithfulness is a sense of the divine in a good day's work, a marriage that reflects the gospel, a financial plan geared toward generosity, an effort to shoot your children into the world, a commitment to growing in Christ, and even a heightened approach to every single normal human interaction you have during the day. This is your calling, wherever you might be, and God is not going to call us somewhere that violates what He's already called us to do.

Living the Call of God

Let's say, for the sake of argument, that you are presented with an opportunity. You believe that work is sacred, no matter how humble, as we considered earlier in the book, and so you approach your decision soberly. Your first question isn't whether or not the new opportunity will advance your career or help you make more money, but whether it is indeed something God is calling you to. One particular is helpful in clarifying this sense of calling: Does doing this work that God *might* be calling you to do violate what you *already know* He's called you to do?

Maybe the opportunity is for a big promotion at work. The salary is good, and you would be advancing further up the corporate ladder. Nothing wrong with that. But when you ask this question, you see that it leads to a host of other questions:

I know God has called me to be a sacrificial husband. Does taking this promotion give me a greater opportunity to do that?

I know God has called me to lead my family and raise my children in His admonition. Do the job requirements make doing so an impossibility?

I know God has called me to not just go to church but be the church. Does taking this job infringe on my ability to serve the local church well?

It might help even more to think of this example in terms of a circle. What that circle represents is God's will for you. And me. And your mom. And your cousin. These are things we know are God's will—for us to be sanctified. For us to be generous. For us to not kill. Things like that.

Now imagine that inside of that circle is another circle, this one representing God's specific will. It's His calling at a given moment. This circle contains things like which college you should go to, who you should marry, and what job you should take. The specific will fits inside the general will of God, not outside of it. That's why the question of whether the work violates what you *already know* God's called you to do is so important. It's because what you *perceive* to be God's call on your life shouldn't contradict what you *know* to be God's call on your life.

Do the Next Right Thing

Armed with this knowledge of what we know is God's call on our life, we can do our jobs. We can be faithful in an age of abandonment. Most of the time, that's much simpler than we might think it is. It boils down to a series of small, boring decisions, made over and over again, day after day.

It means doing the next right thing at any given moment. Our priority should be to do what we know we are to do today, this moment, and not be distracted. We are so bent on the exciting, that we might miss the small choices of faithfulness right in front of our eyes. Those choices might not be easy, but neither are they complicated. Obedience to God in the next thing is the good and right way. There are many distractions, but the calling is clear. Do the next right thing.[4]

It's worth asking the question, sometimes many times each day: What is the next right thing, right now? Is it to apologize to your spouse? Pay those taxes? Take the time to encourage a coworker? Play a game on the floor with your son? Read a book or kill a thought? Give? Pray? Sleep? Don't complicate obedience to God. What is it that you know you need to do now?

A life spent doing the next right thing is not wasted. Obedience isn't always easy, but it's rarely complicated. All we have is today, so take it. Do that which you know is from God, and keep doing it, one choice at a time.

Meteors and Stars

The story of Jim Elliot has been told and retold with good reason: It's an amazing account of unswerving courage and faithfulness to the gospel. He was a standout both academically and athletically during his days as a student and was presented with opportunity after opportunity to go and do most anything he wanted to do. But as his education continued, Jim became convinced of God's will and purpose for his life—to push back the darkness in the world by preaching the gospel where it had never been preached before. So he began his preparations to spend the rest of his life sharing the gospel with the previously unreached people of Ecuador known as the Auca.

Elliot, along with four other missionaries, began making contact with the indigenous people through a loudspeaker and a basket to lower gifts from their airplane. After several friendly encounters, they made plans to visit the people they thought they had befriended.

But on January 8, 1956, the missionaries were attacked and killed by a group of ten warriors from the people they were trying to share the gospel with. Elliot's body was found downstream in the river, along with those of the other men. His life purpose and vision was immortalized by his journal entry for October 28, 1949, which expressed his belief that missions work was more important than his life. "He is no fool who gives what he cannot keep to gain that which he cannot lose."

It's an amazing story that sent ripples through the Christian and non-Christian world. *Life* magazine published a ten-page article about the missionaries. Jim's wife, Elizabeth, not only published two books about her husband but continued the work among the very people who had killed her husband. Thousands upon thousands of people were not deterred by the danger but instead committed themselves to the work of the gospel overseas. Few events in modern history have been used more powerfully by God to send people out into the world for the sake of the gospel.

Perhaps you have heard the story; you may have even read the books or seen the movie. I have; in fact, the quote on the previous page is written on my wall. Jim Elliot's story is a familiar one, but have you heard of Bert? I had not. But by God's grace, I have now, thanks to a message given by Randy Alcorn fifty years after the men died on the beach in Ecuador. Bert is Jim Elliot's older brother. He's the one who isn't famous.[5]

He was a student at Multnomah Bible College in 1949, and he and his young wife were invited by a missionary to come to Peru and join the work there. Other than an occasional furlough, there they have stayed. Now in their eighties, they are still there.

According to Alcorn, if you Google Bert, you find less than seventy entries. But over the years, Bert and Colleen have planted more than 170 churches. And when asked to reflect on his brother, Jim, Bert's response is stirring: "My brother Jim and I took different paths. He was a great meteor, streaking through the sky."

Bert was not. He did not go streaking through the sky. Nobody lined up with their telescopes to watch his life. Instead, as Alcorn puts it, he was the faint star in the distance that faithfully rises night after night, always there. Always faithful. Always doing the same, boring thing.

In the kingdom of God, there is a great need for streaking meteors, but most of us won't be that. We will instead be faint stars—husbands and fathers, wives and mothers. We will be accountants and teachers, business people, and students. We will go through life, day after day, doing very much the same thing tomorrow that we did today.

The important thing for us to remember is that we are needed. There is a great need for people willing to chase the little donkeys of life, not because it's exciting but because they believe in the constant presence and purpose of God. There is a great need for people willing to stand in the midst of the boring, convinced that there is no such thing as ordinary when you follow an ordinary God.

Rise and stand. Then tomorrow, do it again.

NOTES

1. G. K. Chesterton, *Orthodoxy* (London: William Clowes and Sons, Limited, 1915), chapter 4.

2. C. S. Lewis, *The Weight of Glory* (New York: HarperCollins, 2001), 46.

3. Martin Luther King Jr., *Strength to Love* (Minneapolis: Fortress Press, 2010).

4. I'm grateful to Scott Patty, my pastor at Grace Community Church, who has instilled this phrase into my vocabulary.

5. Randy Alcorn's retelling of the story is available at epm.org.

Also available from
Michael Kelley

"Get ready to go on a remarkable journey... Michael Kelley poignantly illustrates the process of turning faith from a noun to a verb and how it can transform and shape our ability to persevere. Everyone needs to read this book."

—PETE WILSON, author of *Plan B* and *Empty Promises*

Visit Michael's Blog at MichaelKelleyMinistries.com
Connect with Michael on twitter @_MichaelKelley